RICH
THINKING
RICH
LIVING

Napoleon Hill (1883–1970), best known for his global bestseller *Think and Grow Rich*, was a self-help author and businessman whose work has influenced millions across the world, from Norman Vincent Peale to Donald Trump. Born poor, Hill lived a colourful life, pursuing several different business ventures and professions. He also met and advised many famous people, such as US President Woodrow Wilson. Hill eventually found widespread success as a motivational author, writing several books on how to achieve success and practically creating the self-help genre.

RICH THINKING
RICH LIVING

NAPOLEON HILL

Published by
Rupa Publications India Pvt. Ltd 2024
7/16, Ansari Road, Daryaganj
New Delhi 110002

Sales centres:
Bengaluru Chennai
Hyderabad Jaipur Kathmandu
Kolkata Mumbai Prayagraj

Edition copyright © Rupa Publications India Pvt. Ltd 2024

All rights reserved.
No part of this publication may be reproduced, transmitted,
or stored in a retrieval system, in any form or by any means, electronic,
mechanical, photocopying, recording or otherwise, without the prior
permission of the publisher.

P-ISBN: 978-93-5702-860-8
E-ISBN: 978-93-5702-933-9

First impression 2024

10 9 8 7 6 5 4 3 2 1

Printed in India

This book is sold subject to the condition that it shall not, by way of
trade or otherwise, be lent, resold, hired out, or otherwise circulated,
without the publisher's prior consent, in any form of binding or
cover other than that in which it is published.

CONTENTS

1. The Limitless Power of the Mind — 7
2. Will You Dare to Explore the Powers of Your Mind? — 15
3. The 12 Riches of Life — 24
4. A Definite Chief Aim — 33
5. Going the Extra Mile — 37
6. Autosuggestion — 57
7. How to Outwit the Ghost of Fear — 60
8. Learn from Adversity and Defeat — 88
9. Maintain Sound Health — 106
10. Peace of Mind and Power of Mind — 120
11. The 17 Principles of Success — 122
12. Golden Rule — 140

1

THE LIMITLESS POWER OF THE MIND

The mind of man would lead all the other Miracles of Life if they had been described in the order of their importance, because the mind is the instrument through which man relates himself to all things and circumstances that affect or influence his life.

Without doubt the human mind is the most mysterious, the most awe-inspiring product which nature has produced, and at the same time it is the least understood, and the most often abused, of man's profound gifts from the Creator.

The mind is the citadel of the soul, wherein is housed the connecting link between the conscious thinking process of man and Infinite Intelligence. It is the switchboard, so to speak, through which man may tune in and communicate directly with the great universal reservoir of Infinite Intelligence, and draw therefrom the answers to all his problems, the way of fulfilment of all his hopes, dreams and aspirations.

And most profound of all, *the mind is the one and only thing over which the Creator has given man the complete right of control; a prerogative which not even the Creator has set aside, reversed or in any manner usurped, which strongly suggests that the mind was intended for man's exclusive use; that it is the most important of all the gifts of the Creator; and the means by which man may control the major portion of his earthly destiny.*

All of man's successes and all of his failures and frustrations are the direct result of the manner in which he uses his mind, *or neglects to use it.*

The functional operations of the mind are divided into nine departments, something on the order of a well-organized business. Some of these departments function automatically, without direction by the individual, while other departments *are under the control of the individual at all times.*

HERE IS A BREAKDOWN OF ALL THE DEPARTMENTS OF THE MIND:

(a) THE FACULTY OF WILL: the Will is the 'big boss' of all the other departments of the mind. Here is the starting point where the individual begins to exercise his Great Prerogative privilege of *exclusive control over his thoughts*. The faculty of the Will is the 'yes' and the 'no' man of the entire mind. It carries out orders of the individual, regardless of their nature or the effect they may have upon the individual. The power of the Will remains strong in exact proportion to its use. An idle Will, like an idle arm, will become soft and weak.

(b) THE FACULTY OF REASON: the faculty of Reason is the 'presiding judge' of the mind. When directed, or permitted, to do so, it will pass judgment on all ideas, aims, desires, purposes and circumstances which the individual brings to its attention; but its decisions can be set aside by the 'big boss', the Will, or offset by the influence of the emotions if the Will does not assert itself. One of the major weaknesses of all so-called thinking is the tendency of individuals to allow their Wills to be set aside by their emotions. This error can be, and it often is, tragic, because the emotions have no relation to logic or reason; therefore, all action growing out of the emotions should have careful attention of the Will.

(c) THE FACULTY OF EMOTIONS: here is the starting place of a major portion of all actions of the mind. People make decisions which harmonize with their 'feelings', and engage in activities which have not been previewed by the faculties of Reason and Will. Such decisions are more often unsound than sound.

The most common reckless use of the emotions, without due attention from the faculties of Reason and Will, originates through the emotion of Love. The emotion of Love partakes of a spiritual quality of the highest order, but it may be, and it often is, the most dangerous of all the emotions because people generally do not submit it to the modifying influence of the Reason and the Will.

Accurate thinkers—people who use all the departments of their minds in the process of thinking—never allow the emotion of Love to express itself until its actions have been carefully looked over by the Reason and the Will. Moreover, the accurate thinker submits all of his deepest desires, plans, and purposes to his departments of Reason and Will *to make sure that his eagerness and enthusiasm do not overthrow his Wisdom*; and his emotion of Love is always under constant suspicion lest it get from under his control.

(d) THE FACULTY OF IMAGINATION: this faculty is the architect of man's soul through which he may pattern his own earthly destiny to suit himself and change or modify that pattern as often as he pleases. With the aid of his Imagination, man may penetrate the interstellar spaces of infinitude with the speed of lightning, conquer the air above him and the seas below him, and create a million ideas and concepts of benefit to himself by merely combining in new ways old ideas and concepts.

Through his Imagination, man may combine fantasy with realism and shape these into living empires of industry which change the entire trend of civilization. Nothing is impossible of accomplishment by the Imagination which is guided by the faculties of Will and Reason, but *unbridled Imagination can play havoc with an individual's life;* and it has been said that when the emotion of Love and the Imagination get together and go on an unchaperoned spree, the individual may never recover from the damage they do.

The Imagination is the place of origin of the sixty-four-dollar physical ailment known as hypochondria, which has proved to be a major problem with doctors. It may also be the place of origin of the cure for hypochondria, and there are many reliable authorities who claim that the Imagination exercises such powerful influence over the physical body that it can activate the body resistance mechanism and cause it to eliminate many types of real physical ailments.

The Imagination is a great institution whose *potentialities are practically unlimited, but it is a very tricky institution which requires constant supervision by the faculties of the Reason and the Will.* It may be helpful if you will read the preceding sentence many times, until you become impressed by the potency of the suggestion it carries.

(e) THE FACULTY OF CONSCIENCE: here we have the department of the mind which gives moral guidance to the individual. If allowed to function without interference, the Conscience carefully processes all of the individual's aims and purposes and warns him when they do not harmonize with the moral laws of nature. This warning ceases and the Conscience eventually goes out of business altogether *if the individual fails or neglects to heed its warnings.*

The individual who has the full support of his Conscience in connection with all his desires, aims and purposes, has direct access to the necessary Faith to enable him to accomplish whatever he may set his heart and mind upon.

(f) THE FIVE PHYSICAL SENSES: the five senses—sight, sound, taste, smell and touch—are the physical 'arms' of the brain, through which it contacts the external world and acquires information. The senses are not always reliable; therefore, they require constant supervision by the faculties of Reason and Will.

Under any sort of highly emotional activity, the senses often become confused and highly undependable, as in the case of sudden fright, or intense anger. No decision which is reached under the influence of fear or anger should be allowed to stand, until it has been thoroughly reviewed by Will and Reason.

(g) THE FACULTY OF MEMORY: here is the 'filing cabinet' of the brain wherein is stored all thought impulses, all conscious experiences, and all sensations which reach the brain through the five physical senses. The Memory is also very undependable, as most individuals can testify. Therefore, it needs supervision and discipline by the Will and the Reason. The main cause for the unreliability of the Memory is due to the fact that the 'filing clerk'—the individual who supervises the action of the Memory—is careless in not having a definite system by which to work.

The Memory can be made reasonably reliable with the aid of a practical Memory training course, such as the Roth system. Reliability of the Memory is entirely a matter of discipline, supervision and education of the 'filing clerk' who is responsible for the function of this important faculty of the mind.

(h) THE 'SIXTH SENSE': this is the broadcasting and the receiving station of the mind through which one automatically sends and receives vibrations of thought, and perhaps other still higher vibrations which emanate on planes of intelligence outside that of our own earth. This is the medium of communication between the individual and the Unseen Guides which are believed to be available for his service.

The 'Sixth Sense' is the medium through which a properly qualified mind may communicate with other minds, at any distance, through the principle of telepathy. The principle of telepathy has been recognized, by reliable authorities, as a workable reality, and the means by which it may be put into service has been described in detail in many books, including some which I have written.

(i) THE SUBCONSCIOUS SECTION OF THE MIND: this is the 'switchboard' through which the conscious section of the mind may communicate directly with Infinite Intelligence. The Subconscious acts upon any idea, plan or purpose which reaches it, and it makes no attempt to distinguish the difference between positive and negative, or right or wrong influences. But it does respond more quickly and effectively to influences which have been highly emotionalized with such emotions as fear, anger, *belief* and *faith*.

The Subconscious section of the mind is amenable to the influences of the conscious section of the mind, which often stubbornly closes the door to the Subconscious through fears and limitations and false beliefs. In order to get around these negative barricades set up by the conscious section of the mind, and in order to give directions to the Subconscious for the cure of physical ailments, doctors of Suggestive Therapeutics often wait until the individual is asleep (sometimes through hypnotism) and then communicate directly with the Subconscious.

As stated earlier, there is a machine in successful operation with which any desired order can be given to the Subconscious while the individual is asleep. The orders or instructions are recorded on a phonograph record and placed on the machine which plays them every fifteen minutes (until the individual awakes and turns off the machine). The machine is operated by a clock which can be set to start the playing of the record after the individual is asleep.

The references in this volume to the departments of the mind are, of necessity, brief and not intended as exhaustive analyses of these subjects, but merely a bird's-eye picture of the 'mechanism' through which the human mind operates, together with a brief description of the extent to which the departments of the mind are under the control of the individual.

I would emphasize that all thought, whether it is negative or positive, sound or unsound, tends to clothe itself in its physical equivalent, and it proceeds to do so by inspiring the individual with ideas, plans and purposes for the attainment of desired ends, through natural and logical means. After thought on any subject becomes, through repetition, a habit, it is taken over and automatically acted upon by the Subconscious.

It may not be true that 'thoughts are things', but it is true that thoughts create things, and the things thus created are strikingly similar to the nature of the thoughts from which they are fashioned.

It is believed by many people, who are competent to judge accurately, that every thought which one releases starts an unending vibration with which the one who releases it will have to contend later; that man himself is but the physical reflection of thought put into motion by Infinite Intelligence. It is also the belief of many that the energy with which people think is but a projected portion of Infinite Intelligence which the individual appropriates from the universal source, through the equipment of the brain.

> The SUBCONSCIOUS MIND WILL NOT ACT
> UPON ANY IDEA, PLAN OR PURPOSE WHICH IS
> NOT CLEARLY EXPRESSED TO IT.

POINTS TO REMEMBER

1. Stop abusing the power of the human mind and use it purposefully.
2. Your mind is the one thing that you have complete control over.
3. The fear itself is always much worse than the thing which is feared.

2

WILL YOU DARE TO EXPLORE THE POWERS OF YOUR MIND?

'You are a mind with a body!'

Because you are a mind, *you* possess mystical powers—powers known and unknown. Dare to explore the powers of your mind! Why explore them?

When you make the discoveries that are awaiting you, they can bring you: (1) physical, mental and moral health, happiness and wealth; (2) success in your chosen field of endeavour; and even (3) a means to affect, use, control or harmonize with powers known and unknown.

And dare to investigate all non-physical forces lying outside the realm of known physical processes—forces which you can use when you learn how to apply them. And this will not be so difficult for you—no more difficult than turning on a television set for the first time.

For a little child can tune into his favourite television program. Now, when he does, he neither knows the construction of the broadcasting station or his receiving set, nor the technology involved. But that's all right. For all the child needs to know is how to turn the right knob or push the right button.

You will see in this chapter how you can turn the right

knob or push the right button to get what you want from the most effective electrical machine ever conceived. Although this particular machine is the sublime handiwork of Divine Power—you own it. How is it made? Well, among other things, it is comprised of over 80 trillion electrical cells. Naturally, it has many component parts. And each part is in itself an electrical mechanism.

And one part is an electrical marvel. Yet it weighs only fifty ounces. Its mechanism consists of over 10 billion cells which generate, receive, record and transmit energy.

What is this wonderful machine that you own? Your body. You are and will be the same *you* even though you lose an arm, an eye, or other parts of your body.

And the electrical marvel? *Your brain and your nervous system.* It is the mechanism through which your body is controlled and *through which your mind functions.*

And your mind: it, too, has parts. One is known as the conscious and the other the subconscious. They synchronize. They work together. Scientists have learned a great deal about the conscious mind. Yet it has been less than a hundred years since we began to explore the vast unknown territory of the subconscious—even though primitive man has deliberately used the mystical powers of the subconscious from the beginning of man's history, and even today the Aborigines of Australia and other primitive peoples do so to a very great extent.

Let's start exploring now!

Day by day in every way I'm getting richer and richer! Let's begin by accompanying Bill McCall of Sydney, Australia on a journey from failure and defeat to success and achievement.

It was at the age of 19 that Bill started a business of his own—hides and skins. He failed. At the age of 21 he ran for Federal Congress. And again, he failed. Now it seems that instead of crushing him, these and other defeats motivated this young Australian to develop inspirational dissatisfaction.

So he began searching for rules of success. You see, Bill McCall wanted to become rich, and he thought he could find rules for acquiring wealth in inspirational books. Therefore, while checking the inspirational book section of the library, Bill became intrigued by the title *Think and Grow Rich*. He borrowed the book and began to read. He read it once, and then he read it again. And even though he read it the third time, Bill McCall was unable to understand exactly how he could apply the principles whereby some of the richest men in the world acquired their wealth. He told us, 'I was reading *Think and Grow Rich* for the fourth time while walking leisurely along a business street in Sydney. And then it happened! It happened suddenly. I stopped in front of a meat market window and glanced up. And in that very fraction of a second, I had a flash of inspiration.'

He smiled as he continued, 'I exclaimed aloud, "That's it! I've got it!" I was startled at my emotional outburst. So was a lady who was passing by. She stopped and looked at me in amazement. I hurried home with my new discovery.'

He continued seriously, 'You see, I was reading Chapter Four entitled *Autosuggestion*. The subheading was *The Medium for Influencing the Subconscious Mind*.

'Now I remember that when I was a boy my father read aloud from Emile Coué's little book *Self-Mastery Through Conscious Autosuggestion*.'

He then looked at me and said, 'It was you who pointed out in your book that if Emile Coué was successful in helping individuals avoid sickness and in bringing the sick back to good health, through conscious autosuggestion, autosuggestion could also be used to acquire riches or anything else one might desire. "Get rich through autosuggestion": that was my great discovery. It was a new concept to me.' McCall then described the principles. It almost seemed as if he had memorized them from the book itself.

'You know: conscious autosuggestion is the agency of control through which an individual may voluntarily feed his subconscious mind on thoughts of a creative nature, or, by neglect, permit thoughts of a destructive nature to find their way into the rich garden of his mind.

'When you read aloud twice daily the written statement of your desire for money with emotion and concentrated attention, and you see and feel yourself already in possession of the money, you communicate the object of your desire directly to your subconscious mind. Through repetition of this procedure, you voluntarily create thought habits which are favourable to your efforts to transmute desire into its monetary equivalent.

'Let me say again: it is most important that when you read aloud the statement of your desire through which you are endeavouring to develop a money consciousness, you read with emotion and strong feeling.

'Your ability to use the principles of autosuggestion will depend very largely upon your capacity to concentrate upon a given desire until that desire becomes a burning desire.

'When I arrived home, out of breath for running, I immediately sat down at the dining room table and wrote, "My definite major aim is to be a millionaire by 1960."'

Still looking at me he continued, 'You mentioned that a person should be specific as to the amount of money he wants and set a date. I did.'

Now, the man to whom we were talking was not the young Bill McCall who failed at the age of 19. He became known as the Honourable William V. McCall, the youngest man ever to become a member of the Australian Parliament; as the former chairman of the board of directors of the Coca-Cola subsidiary in Sydney; and as the director of 22 family-owned corporations. And as to riches—he became a millionaire, and quite as rich as some of the men he had read about in the book from which he got the inspiration *to explore the power of his subconscious mind with self-suggestion.* (Incidentally, he became a millionaire four years ahead of schedule!)

Day by day in every way I am getting better and better! *You will note we use the word 'self-suggestion' as being synonymous with the term 'conscious autosuggestion' used by Emile Coué.*

McCall remembered that when he was a boy his father had benefited from a great discovery found in a book of his day—a discovery that every man, woman and child can effectively employ when he finds it for himself. Like Bill McCall and his father, you too can properly employ the power of conscious autosuggestion.

CONSCIOUS SUGGESTION

Now conscious autosuggestion was revealed to Emile Coué because he dared to explore the powers of his own mind and the minds of others. Before he made his great discovery, he used hypnosis to cure the physical illnesses of his patients. But after making his great discovery, which was in reality based on a simple natural law, he abandoned the use of hypnosis.

And how did he find and recognize this natural law? Emile Coué's great discovery was made when he found the answer to some questions he asked himself. They were:

Question No. 1: is it the suggestion of the doctor, or is it the suggestion in the mind of the patient, that effects a cure?

Answer: Coué proved conclusively that it was the mind of the patient that subconsciously or consciously made the suggestion to which his own mind and body reacted. Without either *(unconscious) autosuggestion* or *conscious autosuggestion*, external suggestions are not effective.

Question No. 2: if the suggestion of the doctor stimulates internal suggestion of the patient, why can't the patient use healthful, positive suggestions on himself ? And why can't he refrain from harmful negative suggestions?

The answer to his second question came quickly: anyone, even a child, can be taught to develop a positive mental attitude. The method is to repeat positive affirmations such as: *day by day, in every way, through the grace of God, I am getting better and better.*

Throughout *Success Through a Positive Mental Attitude*, you will see many self-motivators which you can use for your own self-suggestion. And if by now you don't know how to use self-suggestion, you will before you complete this book.

When death's door is about to open. There are over 450,000 children born out of wedlock in the United States each year, and over a million and a half teenagers enter penal institutions for car thefts and other crimes. These personal tragedies could in many instances be avoided if: (a) the parents learned how to employ suggestion properly, and (b) if their sons and daughters were taught how effectively to use spiritual self-suggestion. Through the proper use of suggestion, these young people could be motivated to develop inviolable moral standards through their own conscious autosuggestion. And they would know how to neutralize or repel the undesirable suggestions of their associates in an intelligent manner.

Of course, every individual responds to *(unconscious)*

autosuggestion throughout his life more often than he does to *conscious* autosuggestion. In such instances he responds to habit and the inner urge of the subconscious. When a man with PMA is faced with a serious personal problem, self-motivators flash from the subconscious to the conscious to aid him. This is especially true in times of emergency—especially when death's door is about to be opened. Such was the case with Ralph Weppner of Toowoomba, Queensland, Australia, one of our PMA Science of Success course students.

It was 1:30 in the morning. In a small hospital bedroom two nursing sisters were keeping vigil beside Ralph's body. At 4:30 the afternoon before an emergency call had been made to his family to rush to the hospital. When they arrived at his bedside, Ralph was in a state of coma as the result of a severe heart attack. The family was now out in the corridor, each one worrying or praying in his own special way.

In the dimly lit bedroom two nursing sisters worked anxiously—one on each wrist—trying to feel a pulse beat. Because Ralph had not come out of the coma during this entire six-hour period and the doctor had done all that he felt he could, the doctor had left the room. He had gone to visit one of his other hospital patients who was also in a critical condition.

Ralph couldn't move, talk or feel anything. Yet he could hear the voices of the sisters. He could think quite clearly during portions of this period. He heard one sister excitedly state:

'He's not breathing! Can you pick up a beat?'

The answer was, 'No.'

Again and again he heard the question and answer, 'Can you now pick up a beat?' 'No.'

'I'm all right,' he thought, 'but I must tell them. Somehow, I must tell them.'

At the same time he was amused at the sisters for being fooled like that.

He kept thinking, 'I'm quite all right. I'm not going to die. But how—how—can I tell them?'

And then he remembered the self-motivator he had learned: *you can do it if you believe you can!*

He tried to open his eyes, but it seemed the more he tried, the more he failed. His eyelids wouldn't respond to the command of his will. He tried to move his arm, his leg, his head—but he couldn't feel any reaction at all. In fact, he didn't feel a thing. Again and again he tried to open his eyes, until at last he heard the words, 'I saw one eyelid flicker—he's still there.'

'I felt no fear,' Ralph says, 'and still thought how amusing it was. Periodically one sister called to me, "Are you there, Mr Weppner? Are you there?" To which I would try to respond by moving my eyelid to tell them that I was all right—I was still there.'

This went on for a considerable time until through constant effort Ralph was at last able to open one, then both, eyes. It was then that his doctor returned. With wonderful skill and persistence, the doctor and nurses brought him back to life.

Hidden persuaders. But it was the autosuggestion: *you can do it if you believe you can*—that he had memorized from the PMA Science of Success course—that helped to rescue him when he was at death's door.

What the mind of man can conceive and believe, the mind of man can achieve with PMA!

You are a mind with a body—a mind, possessing, and also affected by, powers known and unknown! A mind composed of two parts: the conscious and the subconscious.

Here we have stressed most the concept of the subconscious

mind—its powers and the forces known and unknown that affect it. But what about the conscious mind? That is equally important. And you will read about it in the next chapter entitled… *and something more!*

Now, if your reaction to what you have read has not given you an insight on how you can turn the right knob or push the right button to get what you want from the machine you own, dare to explore the powers of your mind.

POINTS TO REMEMBER

1. Exploring the powers of your mind can bring you long lasting happiness and wealth.
2. It is most important that you read aloud the statement of your desire.
3. The potent effect of unseen forces.

3

THE 12 RICHES OF LIFE

The greatest of all riches is…

1. *A Positive Mental Attitude:*
All riches, of whatsoever nature, begin as a state of mind; and let us remember that a state of mind is the one and only thing over which any person has complete, unchallenged right of control.

It is highly significant that the Creator provided man with control over nothing except the power to shape his own thoughts and the privilege of fitting them to any pattern of his choice.

Mental attitude is important because it converts the brain into the equivalent of an electro-magnet which attracts the counterpart of one's dominating thoughts, aims and purposes. It also attracts the counterpart of one's fears, worries and doubts.

A positive mental attitude is the starting point of all riches, whether they be riches of a material nature or intangible riches.

It attracts the riches of true friendship.

And the riches one finds in the hope of future achievement.

It provides the riches one may find in Nature's handiwork, as it exists in the moonlit nights, in the stars that float out there in the heavens, in the beautiful landscapes and in distant horizons.

And the riches to be found in the labour of one's choice,

where expression may be given to the highest plane of man's soul.

And the riches of harmony in home relationships, where all members of the family work together in a spirit of friendly cooperation.

And the riches of sound physical health, which is the treasure of those who have learned to balance work with play, worship with love and who have learned the wisdom of eating to live rather than of living to eat.

And the riches of freedom from fear.

And the riches of enthusiasm, both active and passive.

And the riches of song and laughter, both of which indicate states of mind.

And the riches of self-discipline, through which one may have the joy of knowing that the mind can and will serve any desired end if one will take possession and command it through definiteness of purpose.

And the riches of play, through which one may lay aside all of the burdens of life and become as a little child again.

And the riches of discovery of one's 'other self'—that self which knows no such reality as permanent failure.

And the riches of FAITH IN INFINITE INTELLIGENCE, of which every individual mind is a minute projection.

And the riches of meditation, the connecting link by which any one may draw upon the great universal supply of Infinite Intelligence at will.

Yes, these and all other riches begin with a positive mental attitude. Therefore, it is but little cause for wonder that a positive mental attitude takes the first place in the list of the 'Twelve Riches'.

2. *Sound Physical Health:*
Sound health begins with a 'health consciousness' produced by a mind which thinks in terms of health and not in terms of illness, plus temperance of habits in eating and properly balanced physical activities.

3. *Harmony In Human Relationships:*
Harmony with others begins with one's self, for it is true, as Shakespeare said, there are benefits available to those who comply with his admonition, 'To thine own self be true, and it must follow, as the night the day, thou canst not then be false to any man.'

4. *Freedom from Fear:*
No man who fears anything is a free man! Fear is a harbinger of evil, and wherever it appears one may find a cause which must be eliminated before he may become rich in the fuller sense. The seven basic fears which appear most often in the minds of men are (1) the fear of POVERTY, (2) the fear of CRITICISM, (3) the fear of ILL HEALTH, (4) the fear of LOSS OF LOVE, (5) the fear of the LOSS OF LIBERTY, (6) the fear of OLD AGE, (7) the fear of DEATH.

5. *The Hope of Achievement:*
The greatest of all forms of happiness comes as the result of hope of achievement of some yet unattained desire; and poor beyond description is the person who cannot look to the future with hope that he will become the person he would like to be, or with the belief that he will attain the objective he has failed to reach in the past.

6. *The Capacity for Faith:*
Faith is the connecting link between the conscious mind of man and the great universal reservoir of Infinite Intelligence. It is the

fertile soil of the garden of the human mind wherein may be produced all of the riches of life. It is the 'eternal elixir' which gives creative power and action to the impulses of thought.

Faith is the basis of all so-called miracles, and of many mysteries which cannot be explained by the rules of logic or science.

Faith is the spiritual 'chemical' which, when it is mixed with prayer, gives one direct and immediate connection with Infinite Intelligence.

Faith is the power which transmutes the ordinary energies of thought into their spiritual equivalent. And it is the only power through which the Cosmic Force of Infinite Intelligence may be appropriated to the uses of man.

7. *Willingness to Share One's Blessings:*

He who has not learned the blessed art of sharing has not learned the true path to happiness, for happiness comes only by sharing. And let it be forever remembered that all riches may be embellished and multiplied by the simple process of sharing them where they may serve others. And let it be also remembered that the space one occupies in the hearts of his fellowmen is determined precisely by the service he renders through some form of sharing his blessings.

Riches which are not shared, whether they be material riches or the intangibles, wither and die like the rose on a severed stem, for it is one of Nature's first laws that inaction and disuse leads to decay and death, and this law applies to the material possessions of men just as it applies to the living cells of every physical body.

8. *A Labour of Love:*

There can be no richer man than he who has found a labour of love and who is busily engaged in performing it, for labour is the highest form of human expression of desire. Labour is the liaison between the demand and the supply of all human needs, the forerunner of all human progress, the medium by which the imagination of man is given the wings of action. And all labour of love is sanctified because it brings the joy of self-expression to him who performs it.

9. *An Open Mind on All Subjects:*

Tolerance, which is among the higher attributes of culture, is expressed only by the person who holds an open mind on all subjects at all times. And it is only the man with an open mind who becomes truly educated and who is thus prepared to avail himself of the greater riches of life.

10. *Self-discipline:*

The man who is not the master of himself may never become the master of anything. He who is the master of self may become the master of his own earthly destiny, the 'master of his fate, the Captain of his soul'. And the highest form of self-discipline consists in the expression of humility of the heart when one has attained great riches or has been overtaken by that which is commonly called 'success'.

11. *The Capacity to Understand People:*

The man who is rich in the understanding of people always recognizes that all people are fundamentally alike in that they have evolved from the same stem; that all human activities are inspired by one or more of the nine basic motives of life, viz:

1. The emotion of LOVE
2. The emotion of SEX
3. The desire for MATERIAL GAIN
4. The desire for SELF-PRESERVATION
5. The desire for FREEDOM OF BODY AND MIND

6. The desire for SELF-EXPRESSION
7. The desire for perpetuation of LIFE AFTER DEATH
8. The emotion of ANGER
9. The emotion of FEAR

And the man who would understand others must first understand himself.

The capacity to understand others eliminates many of the common causes of friction among men. It is the foundation of all friendship. It is the basis of all harmony and cooperation among men. It is the fundamental of major importance in all leadership which calls for friendly cooperation. And some believe that it is an approach of major importance to the understanding of the Creator of all things.

12. *Economic Security:*

The last, though not least in importance, is the tangible portion of the 'Twelve Riches'.

Economic security is not attained by the possession of money alone. It is attained by the service one renders, for useful service may be converted into all forms of human needs, with or without the use of money.

Henry Ford has economic security, not because he controls a vast fortune of money, but for the better reason that he provides profitable employment for millions of men and women, and also dependable transportation by automobile for still greater numbers of people. The service he renders has attracted the money he controls, and it is in this manner that all enduring economic security must be attained.

Presently I shall acquaint you with the principles by which money and all other forms of riches may be obtained, but first you must be prepared to make application of these principles. Your mind must be conditioned for the acceptance of riches just as the soil of the earth must be prepared for the planting of seeds.

When one is ready for a thing it is sure to appear!

This does not mean that the things one may need will appear without a cause, for there is a vast difference between one's '*needs*' and one's *readiness* to receive. To miss this distinction is to miss the major benefits which I shall endeavour to convey.

So be patient and let me lead you into *readiness* to receive the riches which you desire. I shall have to lead *my way!*

BE PATIENT AND SEE THE RESULTS

My way will seem strange to you at first, but you should not become discouraged on this account, for all new ideas seem strange. If you doubt that my way is practical, take courage from the fact that it has brought me riches in abundance.

Human progress always has been slow because people are reluctant to accept new ideas.

When Samuel Morse announced his system for communication by telegraph the world scoffed at him. His system was unorthodox. It was new; therefore it was subject to suspicion and doubt.

And the world scoffed at Marconi when he announced the perfection of an improvement over Morse's system; a system of communication by wireless.

Thomas A. Edison came in for ridicule when he announced his perfection of the incandescent electric light bulb, and Henry Ford met with the same experience when he offered the world a self-propelled vehicle to take the place of the horse and buggy.

When Wilbur and Orville Wright announced the perfection of a practical flying machine the world was so little impressed that the newspaper men refused to witness a demonstration of the machine.

Then came the discovery of the modern radio, one of the 'miracles' of human ingenuity which was destined to make the whole world a-kin. The 'unprepared' minds accepted it as a toy to amuse children but nothing more.

I mention these facts as a reminder to you, who are seeking riches by a new way, that you be not discouraged because of the newness of the way. Follow through with me, appropriate my philosophy and be assured that it will work for you as it has worked for me.

By serving as your guide to riches I shall receive my compensation for my efforts in exact proportion to the benefits you receive. The eternal law of compensation insures this. My compensation may not come directly from you who appropriate my philosophy, but come it will in one form or another, for it is a part of the great Cosmic Plan that no useful service shall be rendered by anyone without a just compensation. 'Do the thing,' said Emerson, 'and you shall have the power.'

Aside from the consideration of what I shall receive for my endeavour to serve you, there is the question of an obligation which I owe the world in return for the blessings it has bestowed upon me. I did not acquire my riches without the aid of many others. I have observed that all who acquire enduring riches have ascended the ladder of opulence with two outstretched hands; one extended upward to receive the help of others who have reached the peak, and the other extended downward to aid those who are still climbing.

And here let me admonish you who are on the path to riches that you too must proceed with outstretched hands, to give and to receive aid, for it is a well-known fact that no man may attain enduring success or acquire enduring riches without aiding others who are seeking these desirable ends. To GET one must first GIVE!

I have brought this message in order that I may GIVE!

And now that we know what are the real riches of life, I shall reveal to you the next step which you must take in the process of 'conditioning' your mind to receive riches.

I have acknowledged that my riches came through the aid of others.

Some of these have been men well known to all who will hear my story. The men who have served as leaders in preparing the way for the rest of us, under that which we call '*The American way of life*'.

Some have been strangers whose names you will not recognize.

POINTS TO REMEMBER

1. All riches begin with a state of mind.
2. Find harmony in human relationships.
3. The man who is not the master of himself may never become the master of anything.

4

A DEFINITE CHIEF AIM

Singleness of purpose is essential for success, no matter what may be one's idea of the definition of success. Yet singleness of purpose is a quality which may, and generally does, call for thought on many allied subjects.

A well organized, alert and energetic mind is produced by various and sundry stimuli, all of which are plainly described in these lessons.

It should be remembered, however, that the mind requires, for its development, a variety of exercise, just as the physical body, to be properly developed, calls for many forms of systematic exercise.

Horses are trained to certain gaits by trainers who hurdle-jump them over handicaps which cause them to develop the desired steps, through habit and repetition. The human mind must be trained in a similar manner, by a variety of thought-inspiring stimuli.

You will observe, before you have gone very far into this philosophy, that the reading of these lessons will super induce a flow of thoughts covering a wide range of subjects. For this reason, the student should read the course with a notebook and pencil at hand, and follow the practice of recording these thoughts or 'ideas' as they come into the mind.

By following this suggestion, the student will have a collection of ideas, by the time the course has been read two or three times, sufficient to transform his or her entire life-plan.

By following this practice, it will be noticed, very soon, that the mind has become like a magnet in that it will attract useful ideas right out of the 'thin air', to use the words of a noted scientist who has experimented with this principle for a great number of years.

You will do yourself a great injustice if you undertake this course with even a remote feeling that you do not stand in need of more knowledge than you now possess. In truth, no man knows enough about any worthwhile subject to entitle him to feel that he has the last word on that subject.

In the long, hard task of trying to wipe out some of my own ignorance and make way for some of the useful truths of life, I have often seen, in my imagination, the Great Marker who stands at the gateway entrance of life and writes 'Poor Fool' on the brow of those who believe they are wise, and 'Poor Sinner' on the brow of those who believe they are saints.

Which, translated into workaday language, means that none of us know very much, and by the very nature of our being can never know as much as we need to know in order to live sanely and enjoy life while we live.

Humility is a forerunner of success!

Until we become humble in our own hearts, we are not apt to profit greatly by the experiences and thoughts of others.

Sounds like a preachment on morality? Well, what if it does?

Even 'preachments', as dry and lacking in interest as they generally are, may be beneficial if they serve to reflect the shadow of our real selves so we may get an approximate idea of our smallness and superficiality.

Success in life is largely predicated upon our knowing men!

The best place to study the man-animal is in your own mind, by taking as accurate an inventory as possible of YOURSELF. When you know yourself thoroughly (if you ever do) you will also know much about others. 1(H)

To know others, not as they seem to be, but as they really are, study them through:

1. The posture of the body, and the way they walk.
2. The tone of the voice, its quality, pitch, volume.
3. The eyes, whether shifty or direct.
4. The use of words, their trend, nature and quality.

This philosophy is intended to enable those who master it to 'sell' their way through life successfully, with the minimum amount of resistance and friction. Such a course, therefore, must help the student organize and make use of much truth which is overlooked by the majority of people who go through life as mediocres.

Not all people are so constituted that they wish to know the truth about all matters vitally affecting life. One of the great surprises the author of this course has met with, in connection with his research activities, is that so few people are willing to hear the truth when it shows up their own weaknesses.

We prefer illusions to realities!

New truths, if accepted at all, are taken with the proverbial grain of salt. Some of us demand more than a mere pinch of salt; we demand enough to pickle new ideas so they become useless.

RISKS ASSOCIATED WITH NEW IDEAS

Every person should make it his business to gather new ideas from sources other than the environment in which he daily lives and works.

The mind becomes withered, stagnant, narrow and closed unless it searches for new ideas. The farmer should come to the city quite often, and walk among the strange faces and the tall buildings. He will go back to his farm, his mind refreshed, with more courage and greater enthusiasm.

The city man should take a trip to the country every so often and freshen his mind with sights new and different from those associated with his daily labours.

Everyone needs a change of mental environment at regular periods, the same as a change and variety of food are essential. The mind becomes more alert, more elastic and more ready to work with speed and accuracy after it has been bathed in new ideas, outside of one's own field of daily labour.

As a student of this course you will temporarily lay aside the set of ideas with which you perform your daily labours, and enter a field of entirely new (and in some instances, heretofore unheard- of) ideas.

Splendid! You will come out, at the other end of this course, with a new stock of ideas which will make you more efficient, more enthusiastic and more courageous, *no matter in what sort of work you may be engaged.*

Do not be afraid of new ideas! They may mean to you the difference between success and failure.

POINTS TO REMEMBER

1. Singleness of purpose is essential for success.
2. Exercise your mind just as you do for your physical body.
3. Until we become humble in our own hearts we are not apt to profit greatly.

5

GOING THE EXTRA MILE

Going the extra mile means rendering of more service and better service than you're paid to render, doing it all the time, and doing it with a pleasant, pleasing mental attitude.

One of the reasons why there are so many failures in the world is that the majority of people do not even go the first mile, let along the second one. If they do go the first mile, they usually gripe as they go along and make themselves a darned nuisance to people around them. I suppose you know the type. But it doesn't apply to any of you, because if you were like that before you got into this philosophy, you're going to get over it very fast.

I don't know of any one quality or trait that can get a person an opportunity quicker than to go out of his or her way to do somebody a favour, or do something useful. It's the one thing you can do in life without having to ask anybody for the privilege of doing it. Unless you form the habit of going the extra mile and make yourself as indispensable as you possibly can, the only other way you'll ever be free, and independent, and self-determining and financially independent in old age will be by a stroke of good luck, a rich uncle or rich aunt dying, or something of that sort. I don't know of any way anybody can make himself or herself indispensable *except* by going the extra mile, by rendering some sort of service that you're not expected to render, and rendering it in the right sort of a mental attitude.

Mental attitude is important. If you gripe about going the extra mile, chances are that it won't bring you very many returns. Where do you suppose I get my authority for emphasizing this principle of going the extra mile? Experience.

I've watched the way nature does things, because you won't go wrong if you follow the way or the habits of nature. Conversely, if you fail to recognize and follow the way nature does things, you'll get into trouble sooner or later—it's just a question of time. There is an overall plan in which this universe operates, no matter what you call the first cause of that plan, or the operator of it, or the creator of it. There's just one set of natural laws, and it's up to every individual to discover them and adjust himself favourably to them. Above all, nature requests and demands that every living thing go the extra mile in order to eat, in order to live and in order to survive. Man wouldn't survive one season if it were not for this law of going the extra mile.

Don't render a million dollars' worth of service today and expect to get a bank check for it tomorrow. If you start out to render a million dollars' worth of service, you might have to render it a little bit at a time. You're going to have to get yourself recognized for doing it and you'll have to go the extra mile for a little while before anybody takes notice of you. However, be careful not to go the extra mile *too* long without somebody taking notice of you. If the right fellow doesn't take notice, look around until you find the right fellow who will. In other words, if your present employer doesn't recognize you, fire the employer sooner or later and let his competitor know what kind of service you're rendering. I assure you it won't hurt your chances a bit. Have a little competition as you go along.

Nobody ever accepts a rule or does anything without a motive, and I have a great variety of reasons why you should go the extra mile.

THE LAW OF INCREASING RETURNS

The law of increasing returns means that you'll get back more than you give out, whether it's good or bad, whether it's positive or negative. That's the way the law of nature works. **Whatever you give out, whatever you do to or for another person, or whatever you give out from yourself, comes back to you greatly multiplied in kind.** No exception whatsoever. It doesn't always come back very quickly; sometimes it takes longer than you expect. But you may be sure that if you send out some negative influence, it's going to come back to you sooner or later. You may not recognize what caused it, but it'll come back. It won't overlook you.

The law of increasing returns is eternal, automatic and it's working all the time. It's just as inexorable as the law of gravitation. Nobody in the world can circumvent it, go around it, or have it suspended for one moment. It's operating all the time. The law of increasing returns means that when you go out of your way to render more service and better service than you're paid to render, it's impossible for you *not* to get back more than you really did, because the law of increasing returns takes care of that. If you're working for a salary, the law takes care of it in additional wages, greater responsibilities, promotions or opportunities to go into business for yourself. In a thousand and one different ways, it'll come back.

THE LAW OF COMPENSATION

It doesn't always come back from the source to which you rendered the service. Don't be afraid to render service to a greedy buyer or a greedy employer. It makes no difference to whom you render service. If you render it in good faith and in good spirit, and keep doing it as a matter of habit, it's equally impossible for you *not* to be compensated as it is to *be* compensated. Therefore, you don't have to be too careful about the person to whom you render it. In fact, apply this principle with *everybody*, no matter who it is—strangers, acquaintances, business associates and relatives, too. Make it your business to render useful service to everyone, regardless of the shape, form or fashion in which you touch them.

The only way you can increase the space that you occupy in the world— and I don't mean just the physical space, but also the mental and the spiritual space as well—will be determined by the quality and the quantity of the service that you render. In addition to the quality and the quantity, is the mental attitude in which you render it. Those are the determining factors as to how far you'll go in life, how much you'll get out of life, how much you'll enjoy life and how much peace of mind you'll have.

SELF-PROMOTION

Self-promotion elicits the favourable attention of other people. If you're alert-minded and take notice, you'll find in any organization those people that are going the extra mile. You'll find out very quickly. And if you watch the procedure and the records of those people who are going the extra mile, you'll see that when there are promotions around, they're the ones that get them. They don't have to ask for them; it's not necessary at all. Employers *look* for people who will go the extra mile. It permits one to become indispensable in many different human relationships. It enables one to command more than the average compensation.

GIVING FEEDS THE SOUL

I want you to know that it also does something to your soul inside of you; it makes you feel better. And if there were no other reason in the world why you should go the extra mile, I'd say that would be adequate. There are a lot of things in life that cause us to have negative feelings or cause us unpleasant experiences and feelings. However, this is one thing that you can do for yourself that'll *always* give you a pleasant feeling. And if you'll go back through your own experiences, I'm sure you'll remember that you never did a kind thing for anybody without getting a great deal of joy out of it. Maybe the other fellow didn't appreciate it, but that's unimportant.

It's like love. To have loved, that alone is a great privilege. It makes no difference whatsoever whether your love was returned by the other person. You've had the benefit by the emotion of love itself. So it is by the principle of going the extra mile. It'll do something *to you*. It'll give you greater courage. It'll enable you to overcome inhibitions and inferiority complexes that you've been storing through the years. There is so much benefit available to stepping out and making yourself useful to somebody.

If you do something courteous or useful for somebody who is not expecting it, don't be too surprised when they look at you in a quizzical sort of way, as much as to say, 'Well, I just wonder why you're doing that.' Some people will be a little bit surprised when you go out of your way to be useful to them.

MENTAL AND PHYSICAL BENEFITS

Going the extra mile in all forms of service will lead to mental growth and physical perfection across all areas as well as greater ability and skill in one's chosen vocation. Whether you're delivering a lecture or making up your notebook, or filling your job, if it's something that you're going to do over and over again in your life, make up your mind that every time you do it, you will excel beyond all previous efforts on your part. In other words, become a constant challenge to yourself. See how quickly and how rapidly you will grow if you'll go at it in that way.

I have never delivered a lecture in my life that I didn't intend to deliver better than I did previously. I don't always do it, but that's my intention. It makes no difference what kind of an audience I have, whether I have a big class or a small class. I don't often have small classes, but when I do, I put just as much into a small class as a big one, not only because I want to be useful to my students, but because I want to grow and I want to develop. Out of effort, out of struggle and out of the use of your faculties comes growth. It enables one to profit by the law of contrast. You won't have to advertise that one very much—it'll advertise itself—because the majority of people around you are *not* going to be going the extra mile, and that's all the better for you.

If everybody went the extra mile this would be a grand world to live in, but you wouldn't be able to cash in on this principle as definitely as you can now because you'd have a tremendous amount of competition. Don't worry. I can assure you you're not going to have it. You'll be in a class by yourself. There will be cases where people you work with or are associated with will be shown up for *not* going the first mile, let alone the second one, and they won't like that. Are you going to cry about that one and quit and go back to your old habits, just because the other fellow doesn't like what you're doing? Of course not.

It's your individual responsibility to succeed. That's your sole responsibility. You can't afford to let anybody's ideas, idiosyncrasies or notions get in the way of your success. You can't afford to do that. You should be fair with other people, but beyond that, you're under no obligations to let anybody's opinions or ideas stop you from being successful. I'd like to see the person that could stop me from being successful. I'd love to see what he looks like, and I want you to feel that way about it, too. I want you to make up your mind that you're going to put these laws into operation and that you're not going to let anybody stop you from doing it. It leads to the development of a positive, pleasing mental attitude, which is among the more important traits of a pleasing personality —actually, not *among* the more important; it *is* the most important one. A positive mental attitude is the first trait of a pleasing personality.

It's a marvellous thing to know what you can do to change the chemistry of your brain so that you're positive instead of negative. Do you know how easy it is? It's as easy as getting in that frame of mind where you want to do something useful for the other fellow, without rendering service on the one hand and picking his pocket with the other. You're doing it just because of the goodness that you get *out* of doing it. You know that if you render more service and better service than you're paid to render, sooner or later you'll be paid for more than you do and you'll be paid willingly. That's the way the law works. That's the law of compensation. It's an eternal law, it never forgets and it has a perfectly marvellous bookkeeping system. You may be sure that when you are giving out the right kind of service with the right kind of a mental attitude, you are piling up credits that'll come back to you multiplied, sooner or later.

UNLIMITED BENEFITS

Going the extra mile tends to develop a keen, alert imagination because it is a habit that keeps you continuously seeking new and more efficient ways of rendering useful service. The reason that's important is that, as you begin to look around to see how many places, and ways, and means there are in helping the other fellow to find *himself*, you find *yourself*.

One of the most outstanding things that I discovered in my research was that when you have a problem or an unpleasant situation you don't know how to solve, when you've done everything you know, and when you've tried every source you know of and you're still at a stalemate, there is always one thing that you can do. I want to tell you that if you'll do that one thing, the chances are that you not only will solve your problem, but you'll also learn a great lesson. That one thing is to find somebody who has an equal or a greater problem and start where you stand, then and there, to help that *other* person. Lo and behold, it unlocks something in you. It unlocks cells of the brain, unlocking cells that permit Infinite Intelligence to come into your brain and give you the answer to the solution of your problem.

I don't know why that works, but do you know how I know that it *does* work? Do you know why I can make that statement so positive and not qualify it? I arrived at that decision by experience, by trying it out hundreds and hundreds of times myself, and by seeing it tried out hundreds and hundreds of times by my students to whom I have recommended that same thing. What a simple thing that is! I don't know *what it does* and I don't know *why it works*. There are a lot of things in life I don't know and there are a lot of things you don't know. There are also some things that you do know that you don't do much about. This is one of those things that I don't know anything about but I do something about.

I follow the law because I know that if I need my own mind to be opened up to receive opportunity, the best way in the world to open it up is to start looking around to see how many other people I can help.

PERSONAL INITIATIVE

Personal initiative gets you into the habit of looking around for something useful to do and going out and doing it without somebody telling you to do it. That old man Procrastination is a sour old bird and he causes a lot of trouble in this world. People put off things until the day after tomorrow that they should have done the day before yesterday. Every one of us is guilty of it. I know I'm not free of it and I know you're not, either. But I can tell you I'm freer of it than I was a few years back. I can find a lot of things to do now and I find them because I get joy out of doing them. Anytime you're going the extra mile, you're going to get joy out of what you're doing; otherwise, you won't go the extra mile. It will help you develop the quality of personal initiative and help you overcome the quality of procrastination.

Going the extra mile also serves to build the confidence of others on one's integrity and general ability, and it aids one in mastering the destructive habit of procrastination. It develops definiteness of purpose, without which one cannot hope for success. That alone would be enough to justify it. It gives you an objective, so that you don't go around and around in circles like a goldfish in a bowl, always coming back to where you started with something that you didn't start out with. Definiteness of purpose comes out of this business of going the extra mile. It also enables you to make your work a joy instead of a burden—you get to where you love it. If you're not engaged in a labour of love, you're wasting a lot of your time.

One of the greatest joys in the world is being permitted to engage in the thing that you would rather do than all other things. When you're going the extra mile, you're doing just exactly that. You don't have to do it, nobody expects you to do it, and nobody asks you to do it. Certainly no employer would ask his employees to go the extra mile. He might ask for extra help once in a while, but he wouldn't do it as a regular thing. It's something that you do on your own initiative, and it gives a dignity to your labour. Even if you're digging a ditch, you're *helping* somebody, and there's a certain dignity to that which takes the fatigue and the unpleasantness out of the labour.

Going the extra mile often gives the greatest amount of joy. You might think you go the extra mile being married, but what about before you get married? Believe me, I spent a lot of time burning midnight oil and I didn't consider it hard work at all. It was my own idea and I used my initiative, but I also got a lot of joy out of doing it and I made it pay off. When you're courting the girl of your choice (or being courted by the man of your choice), it's marvellous how much sleep you can lose and still not be seriously hurt by it. Wouldn't it be a wonderful thing if you could put the same attitude into your relations with people professionally or in the business that you put into courtship? We're going to start sparking again.

It's going to start at home, with our own mates. I couldn't begin to tell you the number of married couples that I've started in on a new sparking spree. They're getting a lot of joy out of it. It saves a lot of friction and a lot of argument. It cuts down expenses. Go ahead and laugh, but it will do you good.

I don't mean to be facetious. I'm very serious when I say that there is one of the finest places in the world to start going the extra mile. When you start going the extra mile with somebody that you haven't seen, sit down and have a little sales talk with them. Tell them that you've changed your attitude and you want a mutual agreement for both parties to change the attitude so that from here on out, *all* of us are going the extra mile. We're going to relate together on a different basis, where we'll all get joy out of it, more peace of mind, and more happiness in living. Wouldn't it be a wonderful thing if you went home tonight and had that kind of speech with your mate? It wouldn't hurt; it might help. Your mate might not be impressed by it, but you will be. Nothing will hinder you from enjoying it.

What about that person in business that you haven't been getting along so well with? Why not go in tomorrow morning with a smile and walk over to him or her and shake his hand and say, 'Now look here and listen up, pal. From here on out, let's you and I enjoy working together.' What would he say? It wouldn't work, huh? Oh, yes, it would. You try it and see. There's another thing that we have called pride, and if there's one thing that does more damage in this world than any other one, it's that little thing called pride. Don't be afraid. Don't be afraid to humiliate yourself if it's going to build better human relations with the people that you have to associate with all the time.

'Those final remarks are not in my notes, but I'll tell you where they were: they were in my heart. [Applause.] Thank you. And one of the reasons why you and I get along so well is that very often I deviate from my notes and go down into my heart and dig up things for you that

I want you to have— little morsels of food for your soul that I want you to have, because I know they're good. I know they're good, because I know where I got them and what they've done for me through the years.'

ESTABLISH OBLIGATION

Going the extra mile is the only thing that gives one the right to ask for promotions or more pay. Did you ever stop to think about that? You don't have a leg to stand on if you go to the purchaser of your services and ask for more money or for promotion to a better job unless, for some time previously, you have been going the extra mile and doing more than you're paid for. Obviously, if you're doing no more than you're paid for, then you're being paid for all you're entitled to, aren't you? Certainly, you are. So you have to first start going the extra mile and put the other fellow under obligation to you before you can ask any favours of him. And if you have enough people whom you have put under obligations to you by going the extra mile, when you need some favour, you can always turn in one direction or other and get it. It's a nice thing to know that you have that kind of credit hanging around, isn't it? I want you to have that kind of credit with other people and I want to teach you the technique by which you can do that.

NATURE GOES THE EXTRA MILE

We get our cue as to the soundness of the principle of going the extra mile by observing nature, and there's quite a bit of illustration regarding that. You will see that nature goes the extra mile by producing not only enough of everything for her needs but also a surplus for emergencies and waste. It shows this by the blooms on the trees and the fishes in the seas. She doesn't just produce enough fish to perpetuate the species; she produces enough to feed the snakes and the alligators and everything else. She produces those that die of natural causes, and even more, so there's enough to perpetuate the species. Nature is most bountiful in her business of going the extra mile, and in return, she is very demanding in seeing that every living creature goes the extra mile. Bees are provided with honey as compensation for their services in fertilizing the flowers in which the honey is attractively stored.

But they have to perform the service to get the honey, and it must be performed in advance.

You've heard it said that the birds of the air and the beasts of the jungle neither weave nor spin, but they always live and eat. If you observe wildlife at all, you'll see they don't eat without performing some sort of service, without working or doing something before they can eat. Take a flock of common old cornfield crows, for instance. They have to be organized in order to travel in flocks. And they have sentinels to protect them and codes by which they warn one another. In other words, they have to do a lot of educating before they can even eat safely.

Nature requires man to go the extra mile if he's going to have food. All food comes out of the ground, and if he's going to have food, he's got to plant seed. He can't live entirely on what nature plants (at least not in civilized life). On islands where they're not civilized, I suppose they depend on eating raw coconuts and what have you, but in civilized life, we have to plant our food in the ground. We have to clear the ground first before we plough it, harrow it, fence it, protect it against predatory animals and so forth. All of that costs labour and time and money. All of that has to be done in advance or you're not going to eat. I wouldn't have any trouble at all selling this idea that nature makes everybody go the extra mile to a farmer, because he already knows it beyond any question of a doubt. He knows every minute of his life that if he doesn't go the extra mile, he doesn't eat and he doesn't have anything to sell. A new employee can't start going the extra mile and immediately demand top wages or the best job in the place. It doesn't work out that way. You have to establish a record, a reputation. You have to get yourself recognized and received before you can begin to put the pressure on to get compensation back. If you go the extra mile in the right sort of mental attitude, chances are a thousand to one you'll never have to ask for compensation for the service you render, because it'll be tendered to you automatically, in the way of promotions or increased salary.

LAW OF COMPENSATION

Throughout the whole universe, everything has been so arranged through the law of compensation (and so adequately described by Emerson) that nature's budget is balanced. Everything has its opposite equivalent in something else. Positive and negative in every unit of energy, day and night, hot and cold, success and failure, sweet and sour, happiness and misery, man and woman. Everywhere and in everything, one may see the law of action and reaction in operation. Everything you do, everything you think, and every thought that you release causes a reaction, on somebody else or on you as the person releasing the thought. Because when you release a thought, you're not through with it. Every thought that you express, silently even, becomes a definite part of the pattern of your subconscious mind.

If you store in that subconscious mind enough negative thoughts, you'll be predominantly negative. And if you follow the habit of releasing only the positive thoughts, your subconscious pattern will be predominantly positive, and you will attract to you all of the things that you want. If you're negative, you'll repel the things that you want and attract only the things you don't want. That's a law of nature, too. Going the extra mile is one of the finest ways that I know to educate your subconscious mind to attract to you the things you want and to repel the things you don't want.

It's an established fact that if you neglect to develop and apply this principle of going the extra mile, you will never become personally successful, and you will never become financially independent. I know it's sound because I've had a great privilege that you haven't had yet, but you will have, in time. I've had the privilege of observing a great many thousands of people, some of whom applied the principle of going the extra mile and some of whom did not. I've had the privilege of finding out what happened to those who did and those who didn't. **And I know beyond any question of a doubt that nobody ever rises above the ordinary stations in life or mediocrity without the habit of going the extra mile.** It just doesn't happen. If I had discovered one case, just one case where somebody went on to the top without going the extra mile, I would say then that there are exceptions, but I am in a position to say there are no exceptions because I have never found that one case. I can definitely tell you from my own experiences that I have never had a major benefit of any kind in the world that I didn't get as the result of going the extra mile.

I want you to become self-determining, so you can do these things without the help of anybody. The payoff will come to you when you can go out and do anything in this world that you want to do, and regardless of whether anybody wants you to do it or whether they want to help you or whether they don't, you can do it on your own. That's one of the grandest, most glorious feelings that I know—that whatever I want to do, I can do it. I don't have to ask anybody, not even my wife. But if I had to ask her, I would, because I'm on good terms with her.

PEACE OF MIND

Here's a little item now that's not to be sniffed at: peace of mind that I got out of all those twenty years of going the extra mile. Do you have any idea how many people there are in the world at any one time who are willing to do anything for twenty years in succession without getting something back out of it? Do you have any idea how many people there are in this world who are willing to do something for only three days in succession without being sure they're going to get something out of it? You'd be surprised at how few there are.

We're looking at one of the grandest opportunities that a human being could possibly have, especially here in this country where we really can create our own destiny and where we can express ourselves any way we want. Speech is free, activities are free and education is free. There's wonderful opportunity to go the extra mile in any direction you want to travel in life. And yet, most people are not doing it. I have seen a time when there were not so many people interested in the philosophy because they were prosperous. They were doing all right and they had no troubles to speak of. Today, almost everybody has troubles, or they think they do.

Do you know what I do instead of finding out what's wrong with the rest of the world? Do you know how I put in my time? I try to find out what I can do to correct this guy here. I have to eat with him, sleep with him, shave his face every morning, wash his face and give him a bath now and then. You have no idea how many things I have to do for him! I have to live with the guy, twenty-four hours a day.

I put in my time trying to improve myself, and, through myself, I try to improve my friends and my students, by writing books, by delivering lectures and by teaching in other ways. It pays off very much better than it would if I sat down and took the old newspapers and read all of the murder stories and all of the divorce scandals and everything that's blazoned across the pages every day. I'm still talking about this fellow Napoleon Hill, who didn't have sense enough to decline Andrew Carnegie's offer to work twenty years for nothing. His declining years will be years of happiness because of the seeds of kindness and help he has sown in the hearts of others.

If I had my life to live over again, I'd live it just exactly the way I have. I'd make all the mistakes I made. I'd make them at the time in life when I made them, early on so I'd have time enough to correct some of them. And that period during which I would come into peace of mind and understanding would be in the afternoon of life, not in the forenoon, because I couldn't take it. When you're young, you can take it. But when you pass the noon hour and you go into the afternoon, your energies are not as great as they were before. Your physical energy, and sometimes your mental capacity, is not as great. You can't take as much trouble as you can in your days of youth. And you haven't got so many years left to correct the mistakes that you made.

To have the tranquillity and the peace of mind that I have today, in the afternoon of life, is one of the great joys that has come out of this philosophy. If you ask me what has been my greatest compensation, I would say that's it. There are so many people at my age, and even much younger than I, who haven't found peace of mind and never will. They never will, because they're looking for it in the wrong place. They're not doing anything about it; they're expecting somebody else to do something about it for them. Peace of mind is something that you've got to get for yourself. First of all, you've got to earn it. As to how anybody can get peace of mind, a few of you would be surprised where you have to really start looking for it. It's not where the average person is looking for it. It's not out there in the joys of what money will buy or out there in the joys of recognition and fame and fortune. You'll find peace of mind in the humility of the one individual's own heart.

Engage in at least one act of going the extra mile every day. You can choose your own circumstance, even if it's nothing more than telephoning an acquaintance and wishing him good fortune. You'll be surprised what'll happen to you when you begin to call up your friends that you have been neglecting for some time and just say, 'You were on my mind. I was thinking about you, and I just wanted to call and say how do you do, and I hope you are feeling as good as I am.' You'd be surprised at what that'll do to you and what it'll do to your friend, too. It doesn't have to be a close personal friend. It just has to be somebody you know. Or, maybe relieve a friend from duty for half an hour or so, or have a neighbour send over his children while he attends the movies, or do a little babysitting for one of your neighbours. If you're going to be at home anyway, with children of your own, maybe you know a neighbour who would like to get off and go down to the movies but can't get away from her children. The children may be noisy, and they'll probably fight with your children, but if you're a real diplomat, you'll keep them apart. She'll be under obligation to you, and you'll feel that you've really been kind by helping out somebody who otherwise wouldn't have had a little freedom. It'd be a nice thing for some of you people who don't have any children to say, 'Why don't I come over and baby-sit for you while you go out? You and your husband can go on a little courtship. Let me come over and babysit for you while you go out to the movie or go to a show.' You'll have to know your neighbours pretty well in order to do that. Certainly, most of you would have some neighbour that you could approach on some such basis, and they wouldn't think you were crazy.

It's not so much what you do to the other fellow. It's what you do to yourself by finding ways and means of going the extra mile in little ways. Did you know that both the successes in life as well as the failures are made up of little things? So little that they're often overlooked, because the things that make success are such small and seemingly insignificant things.

I know people who are so popular they couldn't have an enemy. One of them is my distinguished business associate, Mr Stone. He always goes the extra mile and look how prosperous he is. Look how many people are going the extra mile for him. There are a lot of people who, if they didn't make good money working for Mr Stone, they'd pay him a salary just to work for him. I've actually heard one say that he's become immensely wealthy himself working for Mr Stone. He said, 'If I didn't make money out of working for him, I'd pay him if I had to, just for the association with him.' Mr Stone's not different from you or me or anybody else, except in his mental attitude toward people and toward himself. He makes it his business to go the extra mile. Sometimes, people take advantage of that. They don't act fairly with him. I've seen that happen, but he doesn't worry about that too much. In fact, he doesn't worry about anything at all, period. He's learned to adjust himself to life in such a way that he gets great joy out of living and gets great joy out of people. Write a letter to some acquaintance, offering him encouragement. In your job, do a little more than you're paid to do, stay a little longer on the job or make some other person a little happier.

POINTS TO REMEMBER

1. The reason behind the failure of the majority of people is that they give up easily.
2. Nature requests and demands that every living thing go the extra mile in order to eat, in order to live and in order to survive.
3. The eternality of the law of increasing returns.

6

AUTOSUGGESTION

Autosuggestion is a term which applies to all suggestions and all self-administered stimuli which reach one's mind through the five senses. Stated in another way, autosuggestion is *self-suggestion*. It is the agency of communication between that part of the mind where conscious thought takes place and that which serves as the seat of action for the subconscious mind.

The dominating thoughts which one *permits* to remain in the conscious mind (whether these thoughts be negative or positive is immaterial) will *reach and influence* the subconscious mind, through the Law of Autosuggestion.

No thought, whether it be negative or positive, can enter the subconscious mind without the aid of the principle of autosuggestion, with the exception of those thoughts picked up as 'flashes of insight or inspiration'. Stated differently, all sense impressions which are perceived through the five senses are captured and processed by the *conscious* thinking mind and may be either passed on to the *subconscious* mind or rejected, at will. The conscious faculty serves, therefore, as an outer guard at the approach to the subconscious.

Nature has so 'wired' human beings that they have absolute control over the material which reaches their subconscious mind through the five senses, although this is not meant to be construed as a statement that individuals always exercise this control. In the great majority of instances, they do not exercise it, which explains why so many people go through life in poverty.

Recall what has been said about the subconscious mind resembling a fertile garden in which weeds will grow in abundance if the seeds of more desirable crops are not sown therein. Autosuggestion is the agency of control through which an individual may voluntarily feed his or her subconscious mind on thoughts of a creative nature, or, by neglect, permit thoughts of a destructive nature to find their way into this rich garden of the mind.

Many philosophers have made the statement that each person is the master of his or her own earthly destiny, but most of them have failed to say why this is so. The reason that we may be the master of our own earthly status, and especially our financial status, is thoroughly explained in this chapter. We may become the master of ourselves, and of our environment, because we have the POWER TO INFLUENCE OUR OWN SUBCONSCIOUS MIND, and through it, to gain the cooperation of Infinite Intelligence.

The chapter you are now reading represents the keystone in the arch of *The Think and Grow Rich Philosophy*. The instructions contained in this chapter must be understood and APPLIED WITH PERSISTENCE if you are to succeed in transmuting desire into money or any other result you seek.

The actual performance of transmuting DESIRE into money involves the use of autosuggestion as an agency by which you may reach and influence the subconscious mind. The other principles are simply tools with which to apply autosuggestion. Keep this thought in mind, and you will at all times be conscious of the important part that the Law of

Autosuggestion is to play in your efforts to accumulate money through the methods described in this book.

Carry out these instructions as though you were a small child. Inject into your efforts something of the FAITH of a child. I have been most careful to see that no impractical instructions are included because of my sincere desire to be helpful.

After you have read the entire book, come back to this chapter and follow in spirit, and in action, this instruction:

READ THIS ENTIRE CHAPTER ALOUD ONCE EVERY NIGHT UNTIL YOU BECOME THOROUGHLY CONVINCED THAT THE PRINCIPLE OF AUTOSUGGESTION IS SOUND, THAT IT WILL ACCOMPLISH FOR YOU ALL THAT HAS BEEN CLAIMED FOR IT. AS YOU READ, *UNDERSCORE WITH A PENCIL* EVERY SENTENCE WHICH IMPRESSES YOU FAVORABLY.

POINTS TO REMEMBER

1. No thought can enter the subconscious mind without the principle of autosuggestion.
2. Control over the material which reaches their subconscious mind through the five senses.
3. Each person is the master of his or her own earthly destiny.

# 7

HOW TO OUTWIT THE GHOST OF FEAR

Before you can put any portion of *The Think and Grow Rich Philosophy* into successful use, your mind must be prepared to receive it. The preparation is not difficult. It begins with study, analysis and an understanding of three enemies which you shall have to clear out.

These are INDECISION, DOUBT and FEAR!

The Sixth Sense will never function while these three negatives or any one of them remains in your mind. The members of this unholy trio are closely tied. Where one is found the other two are close at hand.

INDECISION is the seedling of FEAR! And remember this as you read. Indecision crystallizes DOUBT. The two blend and become FEAR! This blending process often is slow. This is one reason why these three enemies are so dangerous. They germinate and grow *without their presence being observed.*

The remainder of this chapter describes an end which must be attained before *The Think and Grow Rich Philosophy*, as a whole, can be put into practical use. It also analyses a condition which has reduced large numbers of people to poverty, and it states a truth which must be understood by all who would accumulate riches, whether measured in terms of money or a state of mind of far greater value than money.

Let us now turn the spotlight on the cause and the cure of the Six Basic Fears. Before we can master an enemy, we must know its name, its habits and its place of abode. As you read, analyse yourself carefully and determine which, if any, of the six common fears have attached themselves to you. Do not be deceived by the habits of these subtle enemies. Sometimes they remain hidden in the subconscious mind, where they are difficult to locate and still more difficult to eradicate.

THE SIX BASIC FEARS

There are Six Basic Fears, with some combination of which every human being suffers at one time or another. Most people are fortunate if they do not suffer from the entire six. Named in the order of their most common appearance, they are:

The fear of POVERTY (at the heart of most people's worries)
The fear of CRITICISM
The fear of ILL HEALTH
The fear of LOSS OF LOVE OF SOMEONE
The fear of OLD AGE
The fear of DEATH

All other fears are of minor importance. They can be grouped under these six headings.

The prevalence of these fears, as a curse to the world, runs in cycles. For almost six years, while the Depression was on, we floundered in the cycle of FEAR OF POVERTY. During World War I we were in the cycle of FEAR OF DEATH. Just following the war, we were in the cycle of FEAR OF ILL HEALTH, as evidenced by the epidemic of disease which spread all over the world.

Fears are nothing more than states of mind. But one's state of mind is subject to control and direction.

An individual can create nothing which he or she does not first *conceive* in the form of an impulse of thought. Following this statement comes another of still greater importance, namely, that THOUGHT IMPULSES BEGIN IMMEDIATELY TO TRANSLATE THEMSELVES INTO THEIR PHYSICAL EQUIVALENT, WHETHER THOSE THOUGHTS ARE VOLUNTARY OR INVOLUNTARY. Thought impulses which are picked up by mere chance from sources outside one's own mind (thoughts created in other minds) may determine one's financial, business, professional, or social destiny just as surely as do the thought impulses which one creates by intent and design.

We are here laying the foundation for the presentation of a fact of great importance to the person who does not understand why some people appear to be lucky while others of equal or greater ability, training, experience and intellectual capacity seem destined to misfortune. This fact may be explained by the statement that *all human beings have the ability to completely control their own mind*, and with this control, obviously, all individuals can open their minds to the 'tramp' thought impulses which derive from the brains of others, or else can close the doors tightly and admit only thought impulses of their own choice.

Nature has endowed human beings with absolute control over only one thing—and that is THOUGHT. This fact—coupled with the additional fact that everything that human beings create begins in the form of a *thought*, an IDEA—leads one very near to the principle by which FEAR may be mastered.

If it is true that ALL THOUGHT HAS A TENDENCY TO CLOTHE ITSELF IN ITS PHYSICAL EQUIVALENT (and this is true beyond any doubt), it is equally true that thought impulses of fear and poverty cannot be translated into terms of courage and financial gain.

The people of America began to think of poverty following the Wall Street crash of 1929. Slowly but surely, that mass thought was crystallized into its physical equivalent, which was known as a depression. This had to happen. It is in conformity with the laws of Nature.

THE FEAR OF POVERTY

There can be no compromise between POVERTY and RICHES! The roads that lead to poverty and riches travel in opposite directions. If you want riches, you must refuse to accept any circumstance that leads toward poverty. (The word 'riches' is here used in its broadest sense, meaning financial, spiritual, mental and material estates). The starting point of the path that leads to riches is DESIRE.

Here then is the place to give yourself a challenge which will definitely determine how much of this philosophy you have absorbed so far. Here is the point at which you can turn prophet and foretell accurately what the future holds in store for you. If, after reading what follows, you are willing to accept poverty, you may as well make up your mind to receive poverty. This is one decision you cannot avoid.

If you demand riches, determine what form of riches and how much will be required to satisfy you. You should now know the road that leads to riches. You have been given a road map which, if followed, will keep you on that road. If you neglect to make the start, or stop before you arrive, no one will be to blame but YOU. The responsibility is yours. No alibi will save you from accepting this responsibility. If you now fail or refuse to demand riches of life, it will be because of one thing—the only thing you can truly control—a STATE OF MIND. And a state of mind is something that one *assumes*. It cannot be purchased. It must be *created*.

Fear of poverty is a state of mind, nothing else! But it is sufficient to destroy one's chances of achievement in any undertaking, a truth which becomes painfully evident during any time of economic difficulty and uncertainty.

Fear of poverty paralyzes the faculty of reason, destroys the faculty of imagination, kills self-reliance, undermines enthusiasm, discourages initiative, leads to uncertainty of purpose, encourages procrastination, wipes out enthusiasm and makes self-control impossible. It takes the charm from one's personality, destroys the possibility of accurate thinking, diverts concentration of effort, kills persistence, turns willpower into nothingness, destroys ambition, beclouds memory and invites failure in every conceivable form. It kills love and assassinates the finer emotions of the heart, discourages friendship, invites disaster in a hundred forms, leads to sleeplessness, misery and unhappiness—and all this despite the obvious truth that we live in a world of overabundance of everything the heart could desire, with nothing standing between us and our desires except *lack of a definite purpose and the plans that derive from it.*

The Fear of Poverty is without doubt the most destructive of the Six Basic Fears. It has been placed at the head of the list because it is the most difficult fear to master. Considerable courage is required to state the truth about the origin of this fear, and still greater courage to accept the truth after it has been stated. The fear of poverty grew out of human beings' inherited tendency to PREY UPON OTHERS ECONOMICALLY. Nearly all animals are motivated by instinct, but their capacity to think is limited; therefore, they prey upon one another physically. Human beings, with their superior sense of intuition and the capacity to think and to reason, do not eat other human beings bodily—they get more satisfaction out of 'eating' them FINANCIALLY. Human beings, by nature, are so avaricious that every conceivable law has been passed to safeguard them from each other.

Of all the ages of the world of which we know anything, the age in which we live seems to be one that is most characterized by 'money madness'. People are almost considered less than the dust of the earth unless they can display a fat bank account. But if they have money— NEVER MIND HOW THEY ACQUIRED IT—they are 'royalty' or 'big shots'. They seem above the law, they rule in politics, they dominate in business and the whole world about them bows in respect when they pass.

Nothing brings a person so much suffering and humility as POVERTY! Only those who have experienced poverty understand the full meaning of this.

It is no wonder that people fear poverty. Through a long line of inherited experiences, people have learned, for sure, that some individuals cannot be trusted where matters of money and earthly possessions are concerned. This is a stinging, but true indictment.

The majority of marriages continue to be motivated by the wealth possessed by one or both of the contracting parties. It is no wonder, therefore, that the divorce courts stay busy. So eager are people to possess wealth that they will acquire it in whatever manner they can—through legal methods if possible, through other methods if necessary or expedient.

Self-analysis may disclose weaknesses which one does not like to acknowledge. This form of examination is essential for all who demand of life more than mediocrity and poverty. Remember, as you check yourself point by point, that you are both the court and the jury, the prosecuting attorney and the attorney for the defence, the plaintiff and the defendant—and it is YOU who are on trial. Face the facts squarely. Ask yourself definite questions and demand direct replies. When your examination is over, you will know more about yourself. If you do not feel that you can be an impartial judge in this self-examination, call upon someone who knows you well to serve as judge while you cross-examine yourself. You are after the truth. *Get it, no matter at what cost even though it may temporarily embarrass you!*

The majority of people, if asked what they fear most, would reply, 'I fear nothing.' The reply would be inaccurate because few people realize that they are bound, handicapped, and whipped spiritually and physically by some form of fear. So subtle and deeply seated is the emotion of fear that one may go through life burdened with it, never recognizing its presence. Only a courageous analysis will disclose the presence of this universal enemy. When you begin such an analysis, search deeply into your character. Here is a list of the symptoms for which you should look:

SYMPTOMS OF THE FEAR OF POVERTY

INDIFFERENCE. Commonly expressed through lack of ambition; willingness to tolerate poverty; acceptance of whatever compensation life may offer without protest; mental and physical laziness; lack of initiative, imagination, enthusiasm and self-control

INDECISION. The habit of permitting others to do one's thinking. Staying on the fence.

DOUBT. Generally expressed through alibis and excuses designed to cover up, explain away, or apologize for one's failures, sometimes expressed in the form of envy of those who are successful or by criticism of them.

WORRY. Usually expressed by finding fault with others, a tendency to spend beyond one's income, neglect of personal appearance, scowling and frowning; intemperance in the use of alcoholic, sometimes through the use of narcotics; nervousness, lack of poise, self-consciousness and lack of self-reliance.

OVER-CAUTION. The habit of looking for the negative side of every circumstance, thinking and talking of possible failure instead of concentrating upon the means of succeeding. Knowing all the roads to disaster, but never searching for the plans to avoid failure. Waiting for the 'right time' to begin putting ideas and plans into action, until the waiting becomes

a permanent habit. Remembering those who have failed, and forgetting those who have succeeded. Seeing the hole in the doughnut, but overlooking the doughnut. Pessimism, leading to indigestion, poor elimination, autointoxication, bad breath and a bad disposition.

PROCRASTINATION. The habit of putting off until tomorrow that which should have been done last year. Spending enough time in creating alibis and excuses to have done the job. This symptom is closely related to over-caution, doubt and worry. Refusal to accept responsibility when it can be avoided. Willingness to compromise rather than put up a stiff fight. Compromising with difficulties instead of harnessing and using them as steppingstones to advancement. Bargaining with life for a penny, instead of demanding prosperity, opulence, riches, contentment and happiness. Planning what to do IF AND WHEN OVERTAKEN BY FAILURE, INSTEAD OF BURNING ALL BRIDGES AND MAKING RETREAT IMPOSSIBLE. Weakness of, and often total lack of, self-confidence, definiteness of purpose, self-control, initiative, enthusiasm, ambition, thrift and sound reasoning ability. EXPECTING POVERTY INSTEAD OF DEMANDING RICHES. Association with those who accept poverty instead of seeking the company of those who demand and receive riches.

MONEY TALKS!

Some will ask, 'Why did you write a book about money? Why measure riches in dollars alone?' Some will believe, and rightly so, that there are other forms of riches more desirable than money. Yes, there are riches which cannot be measured in terms of dollars, but there are millions of people who will say, 'Give me all the money I need, and I will find everything else I want.'

The major reason I wrote this book on how to get money is the fact that the world has but lately passed through an experience that left millions of men and women paralysed with the FEAR OF POVERTY. What this sort of fear does to one was well described by Westbrook Pegler in the *New York World-Telegram*:

> Money is only clam shells or metal discs or scraps of paper, and there are treasures of the heart and soul which money cannot buy, but most people, being broke, are unable to keep this in mind and sustain their spirits. When a man is down and out and on the street, unable to get any job at all, something happens to his spirit which can be observed in the droop of his shoulders, the set of his hat, his walk and his gaze. He cannot escape a feeling of inferiority among people with regular employment, even though he knows they are definitely not his equals in

character, intelligence or ability.

These people—even his friends—feel, on the other hand, a sense of superiority and regard him, perhaps unconsciously, as a casualty. He may borrow for a time, but not enough to carry on in his accustomed way, and he cannot continue to borrow very long. But borrowing in itself, when a man is borrowing merely to live, is a depressing experience, and the money lacks the power of earned money to revive his spirits. Of course, none of this applies to bums or habitual ne'er-do-wells, but only to men of normal ambitions and self-respect.

Women in the same predicament must be different. We somehow do not think of women at all in considering the down-and-outers. They are...not recognizable in crowds by the same plain signs which identify busted men. Of course, I do not mean the shuffling hags of the city streets who are the opposite number of the confirmed male bums. I mean reasonably young, decent and intelligent women. There must be many of them, but their despair is not apparent...

When a man is down and out he has time on his hands for brooding. He may travel miles to see a man about a job and discover that the job is filled or that it is one of those jobs with no base pay but only a commission on the sale of some useless knickknack which nobody would buy... Turning that down, he finds himself back on the street with nowhere to go but just anywhere. So he walks and walks. He gazes into store windows at luxuries which are not for him, and feels inferior and gives way to people who stop to look with an active interest. He wanders into the railroad station or puts himself down in the library to ease his legs and soak up a little heat, but that isn't looking for a job, so he gets going again. He may not know it, but his aimlessness would give him away even if the very lines of his figure did not. He may be well dressed in the clothes left over from the days when he had a steady job, but the clothes cannot disguise the droop…

He sees thousands of other people, bookkeepers or clerks or chemists…busy at their work and envies them from the bottom of his soul. They have their independence, their self-respect and manhood, and he simply cannot convince himself that he is a good man, too, though he argue it out and arrive at a favourable verdict hour after hour.

It is just money which makes this difference in him. With a little money he would be himself again.

THE FEAR OF CRITICISM

Just how humanity originally came by this fear, no one can state definitely, but one thing is certain—people have it in a highly developed form. I am inclined to attribute the basic fear of criticism to that part of inherited human nature which prompts people not only to take away the goods and wares of others, but to justify their action by CRITICISM of their victims' character. It is a well-known fact that thieves will criticize those from whom they steal and that politicians seek office not by displaying their own virtues and qualifications, but by attempting to besmirch their opponents.

The Fear of Criticism takes on many forms, the majority of which are petty and trivial. The astute manufacturers of clothing have not been slow to capitalize on this basic fear, with which all humanity has been cursed. Every season the styles in many articles of wearing apparel change. Who establishes the styles? Certainly not the purchaser of clothing, but the manufacturers. Why do they change the styles so often? The answer is obvious. They change the styles so they can sell more clothes.

For the same reason the manufacturers of automobiles (with a few rare and very sensible exceptions) change styles of models every season. No one wants to drive an automobile which is not of the latest style, although the older model may actually be the better car.

We have been describing the manner in which people behave under the influence of the Fear of Criticism as applied to the small and petty things of life. Let us now examine human behaviour when this fear affects people in connection with the more important events of human relationship. Take, for example, practically any person who has reached the age of mental maturity (from 35 to 40 years of age, as a general average), and if you could read the secret thoughts of his or her mind, you would find a very decided disbelief in most of the fables taught by the majority of the dogmatists and theologians a few decades back.

Not often, however, will you find an individual who has the courage to openly state his or her belief on this subject. Most people will, if pressed far enough, tell a lie rather than admit that they do not believe all of the stories associated with a religion, particularly if their religion (or sect) is one of those which are rigidly dogmatic and intolerant of questioning.

Why does the average person, even in this day of enlightenment, shy away from denying his or her belief in those aspects of religious dogma that are almost surely 'fabulous', or fable-like? The answer is 'the Fear of Criticism'. Men and women have been burned at the stake for daring to express their disbelief in ghosts. It is no wonder we have inherited a consciousness which makes us fear criticism. The time was, and not so far in the past, when criticism carried severe punishments—and still does in many countries.

The Fear of Criticism robs people of their initiative, destroys their power of imagination, limits their individuality, takes away their self-reliance and does them damage in a hundred other ways. Parents often do their children irreparable injury by criticizing them. The mother of one of my boyhood chums used to punish him with a switch almost daily, always completing the job with the statement, 'You'll land in the penitentiary before you are 20.' He was sent to a reformatory at the age of 17.

Criticism is the one form of 'service' of which everyone has too much. Everyone has a stock of it which is handed out gratis, whether asked for or not. One's nearest relatives often are the worst offenders. It should be recognized as a crime (in reality, it is a crime of the worst nature) for any parent to create an inferiority complex in the mind of a child through unnecessary criticism. Employers who understand human nature get the best there is in their employees not by criticism, but by constructive suggestion. Parents may accomplish the same results with their children. Criticism will plant FEAR in the human heart, or resentment, but it will not build love or affection.

SYMPTOMS OF THE FEAR OF CRITICISM

This fear is almost as universal as the Fear of Poverty, and its effects are just as fatal to personal achievement, mainly because this fear destroys initiative and discourages the use of imagination. The major symptoms of the fear are:

SELF-CONSCIOUSNESS. Generally expressed through nervousness, timidity in conversation and in meeting strangers, awkward movement of the hands and limbs, shifting of the eyes.

LACK OF POISE. Expressed through lack of voice control, nervousness in the presence of others, poor posture of body, poor memory.

WEAK PERSONALITY. Lacking in firmness of decision, personal charm and ability to express opinions definitely. The habit of sidestepping issues instead of meeting them squarely. Agreeing with others without careful examination of their opinions.

INFERIORITY COMPLEX. The habit of expressing self-approval by word of mouth and by actions, as a means of covering up a feeling of inferiority. Using big words to impress others (often without knowing the real meaning of the words). Imitating others in dress, speech and manners. Boasting of imaginary achievements. This sometimes gives a surface appearance of a feeling of superiority.

EXTRAVAGANCE. The habit of trying to keep up with the Jones, spending beyond one's income.

LACK OF INITIATIVE. Failure to embrace opportunities for self-advancement, fear to express opinions, lack of confidence in one's own ideas, giving evasive answers to questions asked by superiors, hesitancy of manner and speech, deceit in both words and deeds.

LACK OF AMBITION. Mental and physical laziness, lack of self-assertion, slowness in reaching decisions, tendency to be easily influenced by others, the habit of criticizing others behind their backs and flattering them to their faces, the habit of accepting defeat without protest, quitting an undertaking when opposed by others, being suspicious of other people without cause, lacking tact in manner and speech, unwillingness to accept the blame for mistakes.

THE FEAR OF ILL HEALTH

This fear may be traced to both physical and social heredity. As to its origin, it is closely associated with the causes of the Fear of Old Age and the Fear of Death because it leads us closely to the border of terrible worlds of which we know not, but concerning which we have been taught some discomforting stories. Also, certain unethical people engaged in the business of 'selling health' have had not a little to do with keeping alive the Fear of Ill Health.

In the main, we fear ill health because of the terrible pictures which have been planted in our mind of what may happen if death should overtake us. We also fear it because of the economic toll which it may claim.

A reputable physician estimated that 75 per cent of all people who visit physicians for professional service suffer from hypochondria (imaginary illness). It has been shown most convincingly that the fear of disease, even where there is not the slightest cause for fear, often produces the physical symptoms of the disease feared.

Powerful and mighty is the human mind! It builds or it destroys.

Playing upon this common weakness of Fear of Ill Health, dispensers of patent medicines have reaped fortunes. This form of imposition upon credulous humanity became so prevalent some years ago that *Colliers' Weekly Magazine* conducted a bitter campaign against some of the worst offenders in the patent medicine business.

Through a series of experiments conducted some years ago, it was demonstrated that people can be made ill by suggestion alone. We conducted this experiment by causing three acquaintances to visit the 'victims'. Each visitor asked the question, 'What ails you? You look terribly ill.' The first questioner usually provoked a grin and a nonchalant 'Oh, nothing, I'm all right,' from the victim. The second questioner usually was answered with the statement, 'I don't know exactly, but I do feel badly.' The third questioner was usually met with the frank admission that the victim was actually feeling ill. Try this on acquaintances if you doubt that it will make them uncomfortable, but do not carry the experiment too far because some people may actually develop serious physical symptoms in response to suggestion. (There is a certain religious sect whose members take vengeance upon their enemies by the 'hexing' method. They call it placing a spell on the victim, and there are reliable reports that some individuals have actually died after being hexed.)

There is overwhelming evidence that disease sometimes begins in the form of negative thought impulse. Such an impulse may be passed from one mind to another, by suggestion, or created by an individual in his or her own mind.

A man who was blessed with more wisdom than this incident might indicate, once said, 'When anyone asks me how I feel, I always want to answer by knocking him down.'

Physicians sometimes send patients into new climates for their health because a change of mental attitude is necessary. The seed of the Fear of Ill Health lives in every human mind. Worry, fear, discouragement and disappointment in love and business affairs cause this seed to germinate and grow. Every form of negative thinking may cause ill health.

Disappointments in business and in love stand at the head of the list of causes of the Fear of Ill Health. A young man suffered a devastating disappointment in love which eventually resulted in his being hospitalized. For months he suffered a debilitating depression. A psychotherapist was called in. The psychotherapist changed nurses, placing the patient under the care of a *very charming young woman* who began (by prearrangement with the therapist) to coddle him and shower him with affection beginning the first day of her arrival on the job. Within three weeks the patient was discharged from the hospital, still suffering, but with an entirely different malady. HE WAS IN LOVE AGAIN. The remedy was a hoax, but the patient and the nurse were later married. Both are in good health at the time of this writing.

SYMPTOMS OF THE FEAR OF ILL HEALTH

The symptoms of this almost universal fear are:

INAPPROPRIATE AUTOSUGGESTION. The habit of negative use of self-suggestion by looking for and expecting to find the symptoms of all kinds of disease. 'Enjoying' imaginary illness and speaking of it as being real. The habit of trying all fads and 'isms' recommended by others as having therapeutic value. Dwelling on the details of operations, accidents and other forms of illness. Experimenting with diets, physical exercises and reducing schemes without professional guidance. Over-reliance or experimentation with home remedies, patent medicine and quack remedies.

HYPOCHONDRIA. The habit of talking about illness, concentrating the mind upon disease and expecting its appearance until a nervous condition occurs. Nothing that comes in bottles can cure this condition. It is brought on by negative thinking and nothing but positive thought can effect a cure. Hypochondria (a medical term for imaginary disease) is said to do as much damage on occasion as the disease one fears might do. Most so-called cases of nerves come from imaginary illness.

LACK OF EXERCISE. Fear of ill health often interferes with proper physical exercise and results in one's being overweight by causing one to avoid outdoor life.

SUSCEPTIBILITY TO ILLNESS. Fear of ill health breaks down the body's natural resistance and creates a favourable condition for any form of disease one may contact. The Fear of Ill Health often is related to the Fear of Poverty, especially in the case of the hypochondriac who constantly worries about the possibility of having to pay doctor's bills, hospital bills, etc. This type of person spends much time preparing for sickness, talking about death, saving money for cemetery lots, burial expenses, etc.

SELF-CODDLING. The habit of making a bid for sympathy using imaginary illness as the lure. (People often resort to this trick to avoid work.) The habit of feigning illness to cover plain laziness or to serve as an alibi for lack of ambition.

INTEMPERANCE. The habit of using alcohol or narcotics to deaden pains such as headaches, neuralgia, etc., instead of eliminating the cause. The habit of reading about illness and worrying over the possibility of being stricken by it. The habit of reading, listening to or viewing patent medicine advertisements.

THE FEAR OF LOSS OF LOVE

The original source of this inherent fear needs but little description. It obviously (on the male side) grew out of males' early and, apparently, inherently polygamous nature and the propensity to steal the mates of other males. It also derives (on the female side) from woman's maternal instincts and need for protection during periods of pregnancy and early child nurturing. Both men and women, therefore, have a biological and behavioural basis to fear the loss of love or 'mate companionship'.

Jealousy and other similar forms of neurosis thus grow out of human beings' inherited fear of the loss of security that the loss of love and companionship of another person represents. This fear is the most painful of all the Six Basic Fears. It plays more havoc with the body and mind than any of the other basic fears, and it can lead to severe mental problems.

As indicated above, the Fear of Loss of Love probably dates back to the Stone Age, when males stole females by brute force. They continue to do so in modern civilizations, but their technique has changed. Instead of force, they now use the lure of romantic persuasion, the promise of fine clothes, expensive automobiles and jewellery, access to economic power and other bait much more effective than physical force. Males' habits are the same as they were at the dawn of civilization, but are expressed differently.

Careful analysis has shown that women generally are more susceptible to the Fear of Loss of Love than are men. This fact is easily explained. Women through the ages have learned from experience that men, considered as a group, are polygamous by nature, that they are not to be trusted in the hands of rivals.

SYMPTOMS OF THE FEAR OF LOSS OF LOVE

The distinguishing symptoms of this fear are:

JEALOUSY. The habit of being suspicious of friends and loved ones without any reasonable evidence of sufficient grounds. (Jealousy is a form of neurosis which sometimes becomes violent without the slightest cause.) The habit of accusing wife or husband of infidelity without grounds. General suspicion of everyone, absolute faith in no one.

FAULT FINDING. The habit of finding fault with friends, relatives, business associates and loved ones upon the slightest provocation or without any cause whatsoever.

GAMBLING. The habit of gambling, stealing, cheating and otherwise taking risky chances to provide money for loved ones with the belief that love can be bought. The habit of spending beyond one's means or incurring debts to provide gifts for loved ones, with the object of making a favourable showing. Insomnia, nervousness, lack of persistence, weakness of will, lack of self-control, lack of self-reliance, bad temper.

THE FEAR OF OLD AGE

In the main, this fear grows out of two sources: first, the thought that old age may bring with it POVERTY. Secondly, and by far the most common source of origin, thoughts arising from false and cruel teachings of the past, which have been too well mixed with fire and brimstone and other 'bogeymen' cunningly designed to enslave people through fear.

In the basic Fear of Old Age, people have two very sound reasons for their apprehension—one growing out of their distrust of others, who may seize whatever worldly goods they may possess, and the other arising from the terrible pictures of the 'world beyond' which were planted in their minds through 'social heredity' before they came into full possession of their powers of reason.

The possibility of ill health, which is more common as people grow older, is also a contributing cause of this common Fear of Old Age. Eroticism also enters into the cause of the Fear of Old Age, as no one cherishes the thought of diminishing sexual attraction and activity.

The most common cause of Fear of Old Age is associated with the possibility of poverty. 'Poorhouse'—and everything the term conveys—is not a pretty word. It throws a chill into the mind of every person who faces the possibility of having to spend his or her declining years impoverished and worried constantly about meeting both the necessities of daily life and the special needs of old age.

Another contributing cause of the Fear of Old Age is the possibility of loss of freedom and independence, as old age may bring with it the loss of both physical and economic freedom.

SYMPTOMS OF THE FEAR OF OLD AGE

The commonest symptoms of this fear are:

THE TENDENCY TO SLOW DOWN and develop an inferiority complex at the age of mental maturity, around the age of 50, falsely believing oneself to be 'slipping' because of age. (The truth is that one's most useful years, mentally and spiritually, are those between 50 and 60.)

THE HABIT OF SPEAKING APOLOGETICALLY of oneself as being old merely because one has reached the age of 60 or 70, instead of reversing the rule and expressing gratitude for having reached the age of wisdom and understanding.

THE HABIT OF KILLING OFF INITIATIVE, imagination and self-reliance by falsely believing oneself too old to exercise these qualities. The habit of the man or woman of 50 or 60 dressing with the aim of trying to appear much younger and affecting mannerisms of youth, thereby inspiring ridicule by both friends and strangers.

THE FEAR OF DEATH

To some this is the cruellest of all the basic fears. The reason is obvious. In the majority of cases, the terrible pangs of fear associated with the thought of death may be charged directly to religious fanaticism. So-called 'heathen' are less afraid of death than are the more civilized. For thousands of years, human beings have been asking the still unanswered questions, 'Whence?' and 'Whither?' 'Where did I come from, and where am I going?'

During the darker ages of history, the more cunning and crafty were not slow to offer the answer to these questions—FOR A PRICE. Witness, now, the major source of the origin of the FEAR OF DEATH, 'Come into my tent, embrace my faith, accept my dogmas, and I will give you a ticket that will admit you straightaway into heaven when you die,' cries a leader of sectarianism. 'Remain out of my tent,' says the same leader, 'and may the devil take you and burn you throughout eternity.'

ETERNITY is a long time. FIRE is a terrible thing. The thought of eternal punishment by fire not only causes people to fear death, it often causes them to lose their reason. It can destroy interest in life and make happiness impossible.

During my research I reviewed a book entitled *A Catalogue of the Gods* in which were listed the 30,000 gods which humankind has worshipped through the ages. Think of it! Thirty-thousand of them, represented by everything from a crawfish to a man. It is little wonder that people have become frightened at the approach of death.

While the religious leader may not be able to provide safe conduct into heaven, nor by lack of such provision force the unfortunate to descend into hell, the possibility of the latter seems so terrible that the very thought of it lays hold of the imagination in such a realistic way that it paralyzes reason and sets up the Fear of Death.

In truth, NO ONE KNOWS for certain what heaven or hell is like or in what sense either exists. This very lack of positive knowledge opens the door of people's minds to the charlatans so that they may enter and control those minds with their stock of legerdemain and various brands of pious fraud and trickery.

The fear of DEATH is not as common now as it was during the age when there were no great colleges and universities. Scientists have turned the spotlight of truth upon the world, and this truth is rapidly freeing men and women from this terrible fear of DEATH. The young men and women who attend our colleges and universities are not so easily impressed by 'fire' and 'brimstone' any longer. Through the aid of biology, astronomy, geology and other related sciences, the fears of the dark ages that gripped the minds of humanity and destroyed people's reason have been dispelled.

Insane asylums have been filled with people who have gone mad because of the FEAR OF DEATH.

This fear is useless. Death will come no matter what anyone may think about it. Accept it as a necessity and pass the thought out of your mind. It must be a necessity or it would not come to all. Perhaps it is not as bad as it has been pictured.

The entire world is made up of only two things, ENERGY and MATTER. In elementary physics we learn that neither matter nor energy (the only two realities known) can be created or destroyed. Both matter and energy can be transformed, but neither can be destroyed.

Life is energy, if it is anything. If neither energy nor matter can be destroyed, then life cannot truly be destroyed. Life, like other forms of energy, may be passed through various processes of transition, or change, but it cannot be destroyed. Death is a mere transition.

But if death is *not* a mere change, or transition, then nothing comes after death except a long, eternal, peaceful sleep and sleep is nothing to be feared. Either way, you may thus wipe out forever the fear of death.

SYMPTOMS OF THE FEAR OF DEATH

The general symptom of this fear is the habit of THINKING about dying instead of making the most of LIFE, a habit which is due generally to lack of purpose or lack of a suitable occupation. This fear is more prevalent among the aged, but sometimes the more youthful are victims of it.

The greatest of all remedies for the Fear of Death is a BURNING DESIRE FOR ACHIEVEMENT, backed by useful service to others. Busy people seldom have time to think about dying. They find life too thrilling to worry about death. Sometimes the Fear of Death is closely associated with the Fear of Poverty, where one's death would leave loved ones poverty-stricken. In other cases, the Fear of Death is caused by illness and the consequent breaking down of physical body resistance. The commonest causes of the Fear of Death are poor health, poverty, lack of appropriate occupation, disappointment over love, insanity and religious fanaticism.

OLD MAN WORRY

Worry is a state of mind based upon fear. It works slowly but persistently. It is insidious and subtle. Step by step it digs itself in until it paralyzes one's reasoning faculty and destroys self-confidence and initiative. Worry is a form of sustained fear caused by indecision; therefore, it is a state of mind which can be controlled.

An unsettled mind is helpless. Indecision makes an unsettled mind. Most individuals lack the willpower to reach decisions promptly and to stand by them after they have been made, even during normal business conditions. During periods of economic distress (such as the world has recently experienced), individuals are handicapped not solely by their inherent nature to be slow at reaching decisions, but by the influence of the *indecision of others around them* who have created a state of mass indecision.

During an international economic downturn, the whole atmosphere all over the world can be filled with 'Fearenza' and 'Worryitis', two mental disease germs which can spread rapidly. There is only one known antidote for these germs. It is the habit of prompt and firm DECISION. Moreover, it is an antidote which every individual must apply for himself or herself.

We do not worry over conditions once we have reached a decision to follow a *definite line of action*. I once interviewed a man who was to be electrocuted two hours later. The condemned man was the calmest of some eight men who were on death row with him. His calmness prompted me to ask him how it felt to know that he was going into eternity in a short while. With a smile of confidence on his face, he said, 'It feels fine. Just think, brother, my troubles will soon be over. I have had nothing but trouble all my life. It has been a hardship to get food and clothing. Soon I will not need these things. I have felt fine ever since I learned FOR CERTAIN that I must die. I made up my mind then to accept my fate in good spirit.'

As he spoke he devoured a dinner of proportions sufficient for three men, eating every mouthful of the food brought to him and apparently enjoying it as much as if no disaster awaited him. DECISION gave this man resignation to his fate! Decision can also prevent one's acceptance of undesired circumstances.

Through indecision, the Six Basic Fears become translated into a state of worry and anxiety. Relieve yourself *forever* of the Fear of Death by reaching a decision to accept death as an inescapable event. Whip the Fear of Poverty by reaching a decision to get along with whatever wealth you can accumulate WITHOUT WORRY. Put your foot upon the neck of the

Fear of Criticism by reaching a decision NOT TO WORRY about what other people think, do, or say. Eliminate the Fear of Old Age by reaching a decision to accept it not as a handicap, but as a great blessing which carries with it wisdom, self-control, and understanding not known to youth. Acquit yourself of the Fear of Ill Health by the decision to forget symptoms. Master the Fear of Loss of Love by reaching a decision to get along without love if that is necessary.

Kill the habit of worry in all its forms by reaching a general, blanket decision that nothing which life has to offer is worth the price of worry. With this decision will come poise, peace of mind, and calmness of thought which will bring happiness.

Those whose minds are filled with fear not only destroy their own chances of intelligent action, but they transmit these destructive vibrations to the minds of all who come into contact with them and destroy also their chances.

Even a dog or a horse knows when its master lacks courage. Moreover, a dog or a horse will pick up the vibrations of fear thrown off by its master and behave accordingly. Lower down the line of intelligence in the animal kingdom, one finds this same capacity to pick up the vibrations of fear. The vibrations of fear pass from one mind to another just as quickly and as surely as the sound of the human voice passes from the broadcasting station to the receiving set of a radio.

The person who gives expression, by word of mouth, to negative or destructive thoughts is practically certain to experience the results of those words in the form of a destructive kickback. The release of destructive thought impulses alone, without the aid of words, produces also a kickback in more ways than one. First of all, and perhaps most important to be remembered, the person who releases thoughts of a destructive nature must suffer damage through the breaking down of the faculty of Creative Imagination. Secondly, the presence in the mind of any destructive emotion develops a negative personality which repels people and often converts them into antagonists. The third source of damage to the person who entertains or releases negative thoughts lies in this significant fact: Negative thought impulses are not only damaging to others, but they also EMBED THEMSELVES IN THE SUBCONSCIOUS MIND OF THE PERSON

RELEASING THEM and there become a part of his or her character.

One is never through with a thought, merely by releasing it. When a thought is released, it spreads in every direction, but it also plants itself permanently in the subconscious mind of the person releasing it.

Your business in life is presumably to achieve success. To be successful, you must find peace of mind, acquire the material needs of life, and above all, attain HAPPINESS. All of these evidences of success begin in the form of thought impulses.

You may control your own mind. You have the power to feed it whatever thought impulses you choose. With this privilege goes also the responsibility of using it constructively. You are the master of your own earthly destiny just as surely as you have the power to control your own thoughts. You may influence, direct and eventually control your own environment, making your life what you want it to be—or you may neglect to exercise the privilege which is yours to make your life to order, thus casting yourself upon the broad 'Sea of Circumstance', where you will be tossed hither and yon like a chip on the waves of the ocean.

POINTS TO REMEMBER

1. Your ability to use the Law of Autosuggestion will depend largely upon your capacity to concentrate.
2. FAITH is the strongest and most productive of the emotions.
3. Use your power to influence your own subconscious mind.

8

LEARN FROM ADVERSITY AND DEFEAT

No one likes to undergo adversity, unpleasant circumstances or defeat. After careful consideration of real circumstances and the laws of nature, I believe it was intended that we all should undergo adversity, defeat, failure and opposition. People do not like defeat or adversity, and yet I'm compelled to tell you that had it not been for the adversity that I went through during the early part of my life, I wouldn't be standing here talking to you tonight. I wouldn't have completed this philosophy that reaches millions of people all over the world. It was out of the opposition that I met with that I grew the strength, the wisdom, and the ability to complete this philosophy and take it to the people in the shape that it's in now.

If had my choice, there's no doubt that I would have made it easier for myself, just the same as you would from here on out. We're all inclined to find the line of less resistance. Did you know that picking the line of less resistance is what makes all rivers, and some men, crooked? That's right, yet it's a very common habit for us to do that. We don't want to pay the price of intense effort, no matter what we're doing. We like to have things come the easy way. The mind is just like any other part of the physical body. It atrophies, withers away and becomes weak through disuse. One of the best things that can happen to you is to meet with problems, circumstances and incidents that force you to think, because without a motive, you might not do much thinking anyway.

FORTY MAJOR REASONS FOR FAILURE

There are forty major reasons or causes of failure—more than twice as many causes of failure as there are principles of success. There are seventeen principles of success, some combination of which is responsible for all successful achievements, and more than forty major causes of failure. The forty I talk about are not all of them; they're just the major causes.

IMPORTANCE OF KNOWING YOUR WEAKNESS

Self-examination is one of the most profitable things that you can indulge in. Sometimes you don't want to do it but it's a very necessary thing for us to know ourselves as we are—especially our weaknesses.

In sharing this philosophy of success, it is necessary to tell you the things that you should do and also the things you should not do. Grade yourself as I go along and comment on each one of them. Grade yourself from zero to one hundred. If you're 100 per cent free of any one of them, grade yourself 100 per cent. If you're only 50 per cent free, grade yourself 50 per cent. And if you aren't free at all, grade yourself 0. When you're through, add the total and divide it by forty to get your general average on controlling the things that cause men and women to fail.

1. DRIFTING WITHOUT DEFINITE PLANS
If you don't follow that habit of drifting, if you make decisions

quickly, lay out plans and follow those plans, know exactly where you're going and are on the way, you can grade yourself 100 per cent on this one. However, be careful before you mark your grade, because it's the rarest thing in the world that anybody would grade himself 100 per cent on this one. To do that, you really have to be organized and you really have to be prepared.

2. PHYSICAL HANDICAP

I may not need to make any comment about an unfavourable hereditary foundation at birth. On the other hand, it could be a cause of failure, or it could also be a cause of success. Some of the most successful people I have ever known were handicapped by bad afflictions at birth.

3. MEDDLESOME CURIOSITY

Without curiosity, we'd never learn anything; we'd never investigate anything. But the wording, as 'meddlesome curiosity', involves other people's affairs, something that doesn't really concern you, right? If you're not guilty of that, you'll grade yourself 100 per cent. Or will you? As you grade yourself, go back to your past experiences and determine to what extent you have control of this weakness.

4. LACK OF PURPOSE

Lack of purpose specifically refers to lacking a definite major purpose as a lifetime goal. If you lack this, here's a mighty good place to rate yourself 0.

5. INADEQUATE EDUCATION

One of the most astounding things that I have discovered is that there is very little relationship between schooling and success. I want you to think about that one. Some of the most successful people I have ever known have been people with the least amount of formal education or formal schooling.

A lot of people kid themselves into believing that they're failures because they don't have a college education. If you come out of college with the feeling that you should be paid for what you know instead of what you do, then that college education hasn't done you much good. Wait until you meet that old man destiny standing just around the corner with a club (and it's not stuffed with cotton). Sooner or later, you'll find out that you're not going to be paid for *what you know*, you're going to be paid for *what you do with what you know* or *what you can get other people to do.*

6. LACK OF SELF-DISCIPLINE
Lack of self-discipline is generally manifested by excesses in eating, drinking and indifference toward opportunities for self-advancement and improvement. Lack of self-discipline. I hope you can grade yourself very high on this one.

7. LACK OF AMBITION
Lack of ambition is an inability to aim above mediocrity. How much ambition do you have? Where are you going in life, what do you want out of life, and what are you going to settle for? There was a young soldier I came across just after World War I who said he just wanted a sandwich and a place to sleep that night, but I wouldn't let him do it. I talked him into settling for a higher rate than that, and the result was that he became a multimillionaire within the next four years. I hope I'll have as much success with you in stepping your ambition up to where you're not willing to settle for a penny. Aim high. It's not going to cost you anything to aim high. You may not get as far as you aim, but you can certainly get farther than if you don't aim at all. Get your sights raised up. Be ambitious and be determined that you're going to become in the future what you have failed

to become in the past.

8. POOR HEALTH

Ill health is often due to wrong thinking and improper diet. People have a lot of alibis on account of ill health, I can assure you. They have a lot of imaginary ailments (they call it hypochondria in the Materia Medica). I don't know to what extent you've been coddling or babying yourselves on this, that, and the other imaginary aliments. If you have, grade yourself pretty low on that one.

9. UNFAVOURABLE CHILDHOOD

What about unfavourable environmental influences during childhood? Once in a great while you'll find that the influences upon a person during childhood are of such a negative nature that a person will go all the way through life with those negative influences. I'm quite convinced that if I had been permitted to continue in my childhood as I started out, before my stepmother came into the picture, I really and truly would have become a second Jesse James—only I would have been able to shoot faster and straighter than he did.

10. LACK OF PERSISTENCE

Lack of persistence is failing to follow through with one's duties. What is it that causes people to fail to follow through when they start something? What's the main reason why people do not follow through, do the thing right and see that it's done right? Lack of motive, that's the answer. They don't want to do it badly enough. I'll follow through on anything that I want to follow through on, but if I don't want to follow through, I can find a lot of alibis to keep from doing it. Is it profitable for you to get in the habit of following through when you undertake something, or is it profitable to permit yourself to be side-tracked? How do you rate on that one? Do you follow through or are you easily side-tracked? Are you easily dissuaded from doing a thing when somebody criticizes you? Believe me, if I had been afraid of criticism, I never would have gotten anywhere in life. In fact, I got to where I really courted criticism because it put the fight in me; when that fight was in me, I did a much better job and I carried through better.

There are a lot of people who fail because they lack that driving force that causes them to carry through, especially when the going is hard. No matter what you're doing, you're going to run into that period when the going is hard. If it's a new business, you'll probably need finances you don't have in the beginning. If it's a profession, you'll need clients you don't have in the beginning. If it's a new job, you'll need recognition with your employer that you don't have—you have to earn that recognition. You need follow-through in the beginning, when the going is always hard.

11. NEGATIVE ATTITUDE

People can have a habit of negative mental attitude, a habit of keeping their mind negative all the time. Are you preponderantly negative most of the time or are you preponderantly positive? When you see a doughnut, what do you see first? Is the first thing you see the hole or the doughnut? Of course, you don't eat the hole, you just eat the doughnut. But a lot of people who come across a problem are like the fellow who sees the hole in the doughnut and growls about it because it takes out so much cake. They don't see the doughnut itself. This is a negative mental attitude.

What is the result of a person who has the habit of allowing his mind to become negative and remain negative? You can't put him in jail for it. You can't sue him for it. A negative mind repels people. A positive mind attracts...what? It attracts people who harmonize with your positive mental attitude and your fine character. Just like that old saying, 'Birds of a feather flock together,' negative birds flock to the negative mind, and positive birds flock to the positive mind.

Who has control over your mind? Who determines whether it's positive or negative? I want you to grade yourself on the extent to which you exercise that prerogative—the most precious thing you have or ever will have. The only thing you have complete unchallenged control over is the right to make your mind positive and keep it that way, or allow the circumstances of life to make it negative. You have to work to keep your mind positive. Why? With so many negative influences around you—so many people, so many circumstances—you'll become negative if you let yourself become a part of those circumstances instead of creating your own in your mind. If you have a very clear concept of the difference between a negative mind and a positive mind, can you picture what happens in the chemistry of the brain when your mind is positive or when it's negative? Have you noticed the difference between your achievements when you are afraid and the achievements when you are not afraid (whether in selling, teaching, lecturing, writing or anything else)?

I first wrote *Think and Grow Rich* while I was working for President Roosevelt during that bad depression, which was during his first term. I wrote it in that same negative mental attitude that everybody else was in (in other words, my negative attitude was unconsciously forced upon me by the masses). Several years later when I got that book out and read it, I recognized it was not a saleable book because of its being negative. A reader will pick up exactly the mental attitude that a writer is in when he writes a book, no matter what kind of language or terminology he uses. Without changing a word in the book, I sat down at my typewriter when I was in a new frame of mind. I was 'up on the beam', as we say—100 per cent positive—and I typed that book in *that* frame of mind and that's the thing that made that book click. You can't afford to do anything when you're negative. Anything you do that you expect to benefit you, anything that you expect to influence other people—if you want to get people to cooperate with you, if you want to sell people something, or if you want to make a good impression upon people, don't come near them until you're in a positive frame of mind.

Grade yourself accurately on this one. Grade yourself on the *average* state of mind that you maintain, not just on your state of mind at any given time. Here's a good rule to go by to determine whether or not you are more positive than you are negative: observe how you feel when you wake up in the morning and get out of bed. If you're not in a good frame of mind, I can tell you it's because a lot of thought habits that preceded that hour (the day before, perhaps) had been negative. You can make yourself very ill by allowing your mind to become negative and it will reflect itself the next morning. When you come out of sleep, you're just fresh from coming out of the influence of your subconscious mind. Your conscious mind had been off duty all night, and when it goes back on duty, it finds a mess there that you've got to clean up. But, the subconscious mind's been stirring all night long. If you wake up full of joy and you want to get going on what you're going to do today, chances are you've been pretty positive the day before, or maybe several days before.

12. UNCONTROLLED EMOTIONS
Emotions are both negative and positive. Have you ever realized

that it's just as necessary to control your positive emotions as it is your negative ones? Why? Why in the world would I want to control the emotion of love, for instance? One woman answered, 'Love can get you in hot water. It can *scald* you.' (She must have had some experience with that.) How about the emotional desire for financial gain? Do you need to control the desire for money? You're not afraid of getting too much, are you? Maybe getting it the *wrong* way, or working your emotion up to where you want to get *too* much. I met a lot of people who had too much money for their own good, especially people who got it without earning it or people who inherited it.

Would you be interested in knowing why they call me Napoleon? I'm going to tell you because it makes a good point here. Since I was the eldest son (or the first child), my father named me after my great-uncle, Napoleon Hill, of Memphis, Tennessee, who was a multimillionaire cotton broker. I suppose my father hoped that when Uncle Napoleon died, I would get some of the money. Well, he died and I didn't get any of the money, and when I found out that I was not going to get any of it, I felt very bad. After I swapped some of my youth for wisdom and observed what happened to the ones who *did* get it, I was thankful—eternally grateful—that I didn't get a dime of it because I learned a better way of getting it for myself than having it given to me.

13. SOMETHING FOR NOTHING

The desire for something for nothing, or the desire for something for less than its value, is actually the desire for something without being willing to give adequate compensation for it. Are you ever troubled with that tendency? Who of us hasn't been at one time or another? You can have a lot of faults, but you want to find out what they are and start getting rid of them —that's why we're making this analysis. This is your chance to come face-to-face, be trial judge, defendant and prosecutor all at one time. You get to make the final decision. Far better for you to find your faults than it would be for me to find them for you. Because if you find them, you're not going to spend any alibis; you're going to try get rid of them.

14. INABILITY TO MAKE DECISIONS

Do you have a habit of reaching decisions promptly and firmly? Or do you reach decisions very slowly, and after you reach them, do you allow the first person that comes along to reverse you? Do you allow circumstances to reverse your decision without a sound reason? To what extent do you stand by your decisions after you make them? What circumstances would cause you to reverse a decision you made?

You should hold an open mind on that subject at all times. Never make a decision and say, 'That's it and I'm going to stand by it forever,' because something might develop later on that would prompt you to reverse that decision. Some people are stubborn. Right or wrong, once they've made a decision, they die by it. I've seen a lot of people who would rather die than reverse themselves or have somebody reverse them on a decision. Of course you're not like that. Not if you're really indoctrinated with this philosophy. You may have behaved like that once, but you're not like that now (or you're not going to be like that after this).

15. EXCESSIVE WORRY

This is a wonderful world we're living in. I'm glad I'm here. I'm glad I'm doing what I am, and if unpleasant circumstances cross my path, I am very glad for that, too, because I'll find out whether I'm stronger than the circumstances or not. As long as I can conquer them and go over them, I'm not going to worry about circumstances. I won't worry about things that oppose me; people that don't like me, people who say mean things about me. I'd worry if people said mean things about me and, after examining myself, found out they were telling the truth. As long as they're not telling the truth, I can stand back and laugh at them for how foolish they are and how much damage they're doing to themselves.

16. POOR CHOICE OF SPOUSE

He2re's a honey: number sixteen—the wrong selection of a mate in marriage. Don't be too quick to grade yourself on that one. If you made a 100 per cent mistake on that, look around before you grade yourself and see if you can't do something about correcting that mistake, maybe resell yourself. I've known of that being done, haven't you? There are some people who believe all marriages are made in heaven, and it'd be a wonderful thing if they were, but I've seen some that were not made in heaven. I don't know where else they might have been made, but they certainly weren't made in heaven.

I've also seen business marriages or business relationships that were not made in heaven, and I've helped to correct a lot of those in which business associates weren't working together in a spirit of harmony. Believe me, no business on the face of this earth can succeed unless the people at the top level, at least, are working in harmony.

There's no household or home that can be a joy, or a place that you want to go, unless there is harmony at the top. That harmony starts with loyalty, dependability and ability. That's how I'd evaluate people. If I want to select a man or woman for a high position, the first thing I would look for is whether that person was loyal to the people to whom he owed loyalty. If they didn't have loyalty, I wouldn't want him or her on any terms whatsoever. The next thing I would look for would be dependability, whether or not you can depend upon him to be at the right place at the right time and to do the right thing. After that would come ability. I've seen a lot of people who had great ability but they were not dependable, not loyal and, therefore, very dangerous.

17. OVERLY CAUTIOUS

Number seventeen is having overcaution in business and professional relationships. Have you seen people so cautious that they wouldn't trust their own mother-in-law? I knew a man who was so cautious that he had a special wallet made with a little lock put on it. He hid the key in a different place every night, so that his wife couldn't go through his trousers and take money out of his wallet. Wasn't he a honey? I bet his wife loved him.

This is about overcaution in business and professional relationship, and lack of all forms of caution in all human relationships. Have you seen people like that? They just didn't have any caution. Some people start their mouths going and go off and leave them. Never mind what they're going to say, nor what the effect will be on other people. You've seen people like that, haven't you? They have no caution whatsoever—no discrimination, diplomacy or consideration of what they do to other people through their words. I've seen people with tongues that were sharper than an unused double-edged Gillette blade. I've seen people who would sign anything a salesman put in front of them, not even reading it. They wouldn't even read the big type, let alone the little type. Have you seen people like that?

Of course you're not like that. You know you can be overcautious and you can be under-cautious. The happy medium is found in the lesson on accurate thinking where you carefully examine things you are going to do before you do them, not afterward, and where you evaluate your words before you express them, not afterward.

18. OVERLY TRUSTING

I know it might be a little bit difficult for you to grade yourselves accurately on this one. To be perfectly candid with you, it would be a little difficult for me to grade myself accurately on seventeen and eighteen, because there've been a lot of times in my life when I wasn't cautious at all. I think most of my troubles in my early days came through my trusting too many people. I let somebody come along and flatter me into using the name Napoleon Hill, and he'd go out and flim-flam a lot of people—all in the name of Napoleon Hill. That happened several times in my life before I tightened up and became cautious. That can happen to a lot of people you know, but on the other hand, I wouldn't want to become so cautious that I didn't trust anybody for anything. You'd get no joy out of living if you did that.

19. POOR CHOICE OF ASSOCIATES

How many times have you heard of people getting into trouble because they were associated with the wrong kind of people? I've never seen a youngster in my life that became bad or went wrong, where the reason couldn't be traced back to the influence of some other person. Not once have I ever known a youngster to go wrong or to get into bad habits unless somebody else influenced them.

20. WRONG VOCATION

Number twenty is the wrong selection of a vocation or a total neglect of a choice of a vocation. About ninety-eight people out of every hundred would grade 0 on that one. Of course, students of this philosophy who have been indoctrinated by lesson number one on definite major purpose would grade much higher than that. Give yourself a grade 0 or 100 per cent on this one, not halfway. You either have a definite major purpose or you don't have it. You can't grade 50 or 60 or any other amount on this one, or on definiteness of purpose. You either have a major purpose or you don't have it.

21. LACK OF CONCENTRATION

Lack of concentration of effort is like having divided interests. You don't split your interests or divide them over a lot of different things. One person is not strong enough to do this. Life is too short to ensure your success unless you learn the art of concentrating everything you've got on one thing at a time. You also have to follow through on that one thing and do a good job.

22. FAILURE TO BUDGET MONEY

It might be difficult for you to grade yourself on number twenty-two: lack of a budget, control over income and expenditures and having a systemic way of taking care of your income and your expenditures. Do you know how the average person manages the question of a budget? He manages it by being well over on his expenditures, depending on the amount of credit that he can get from other people. When the credit shuts down on him, then he more or less slacks off, but until that happens, he'll run wild with spending.

A good business firm would go bankrupt quickly if they didn't have a system of control over income and expenditures. That's what a comptroller in an organization is for. (Usually called a wet blanket, every successful business of any size has to have a wet blanket.) A man who controls the assets of the company keeps the numbers from getting away at the wrong time and the wrong way.

23. FAILURE TO BUDGET TIME

Time is the most precious thing that you have. Of the twenty-four hours in every day, each person generally devotes eight hours to sleep, eight hours to make a living and another eight hours to free time.

As Americans, we have the freedom to do anything we want with those 'free' eight hours. You can sin, spend, establish good habits or bad habits, re-educate yourself and so forth. But what are you actually doing with those eight hours? That's going to be the determining factor on how you grade yourself on this particular question. Are you budgeting the use of your time to the best advantage? Do you have a system of actually making all of your time count? The first sixteen hours is taken care of automatically, but the other eight hours is not. It's flexible and you can do what you want with it.

24. LACK OF ENTHUSIASM

Without doubt, enthusiasm is among the most valuable emotions, provided that you can turn it on and off, like a water spigot or an electric light. If you can turn on your enthusiasm when you want to and turn it off whenever you want to, you can grade yourself 100 per cent on this one. Lack of the ability to do that would grade you somewhere toward that little zero.

How do you go about controlling your enthusiasm? Have you ever thought about your willpower? What it was placed there for? You have a power of will and what's the purpose of that power of will? It's for discipline to make your mind whatever you want it to be and form whatever habits you want.

I have never been able to determine in my own mind which is worse: no enthusiasm at all (like a cold fish), or red-hot enthusiasm (that's out of control). They're both bad.

If somebody made me mad right now, I could turn off my enthusiasm just like that and turn on something else. That might be much more appropriate (provided that I kept bad language out of the picture, that is). But there was a time when I could turn on the anger much more quickly than I could turn on enthusiasm, and I couldn't turn off anger nearly as easily. That's something you will have to overcome, the ability to turn on or turn off any of your emotions.

25. INTOLERANCE

Intolerance is a closed mind based on ignorance or prejudice, in connection with religious, racial, political and economic ideas. How do you rate on that one? It would be a marvellous thing if you could rate 100 per cent and honestly say that you have an open mind on all subjects, and toward all people, at all times. However, if you could say that, you'd probably not be human—you'd be a saint.

I suppose there are times when you can make up your mind to be openminded on all these things, at least for a little while. I know I can, at least for a little while. However, if you can't grade 100 per cent, and can't honestly say you are openminded toward all people, at all times, on all subjects, what is the next best thing to do? We're tolerant some of the time, of course. The more you try to be tolerant, you'll eventually get to where you'll be in the habit of tolerance instead of intolerance.

When the vast majority of people meet other people, they immediately begin to look for the things that they don't like in the other people, and they *always* find things they don't like. But there's another type of person, and I notice that this other type of person is always much more successful, much more happy, and much more welcome when he comes around, or when he meets a person. Whether it's an acquaintance or a stranger, the first thing he does is not only to look for things that he likes in that person, but also to compliment them, either by saying or doing something to indicate that he recognizes their good qualities (instead of the bad ones). I get a great feeling when somebody walks up to me and says, 'Aren't you Napoleon Hill?' and I say, 'Yes, I'm guilty.' 'Well, I want to tell you, Mr Hill, how much good I got out of your book. I just thrive on it, I love it, and it does me a lot of good.' I enjoy it, unless of course they rub it on too thick (and you can do that too, you know). My point is, I've never seen the person that doesn't respond in kind if you compliment that person. As bad natured as they are, even a pussycat will curl up his tail and begin to purr if you stroke him on the back. Cats are not very friendly, but you can make them friendly if you do what cats like.

26. UNCOOPERATIVE

Uncooperative means failure to cooperate with others in the spirit of harmony. I suppose there are circumstances in which failure to cooperate would be justified. Or are there? There are a lot of circumstances where you fail to cooperate. I often come into contact with people who want me to do things that I can't possibly do for them. They want my influence, want me to write letters of recommendation or want me to make telephone calls for them. I don't do any of those things, or cooperate in any way, unless I'm sold on what I'm cooperating with, and with whom I'm cooperating. You might want to be like that, too.

27. UNEARNED RICHES

Do you have possession of power or wealth not based on merit or what you've earned? I hope you won't have any trouble grading yourself on this one.

28. LACK OF LOYALTY

Another reason for failure is that lack of a spirit of loyalty for those to whom it is due. If you have loyalty in your heart to those to whom loyalty is due, perhaps you can grade 100 per cent. Unless you practice that all the time, you wouldn't grade 100 per cent; you would grade something lower than that.

POINTS TO REMEMBER

1. Do not accept defeat as failure but only as a temporary event that may prove to be a blessing in disguise.
2. Instead of focusing on your setbacks, maintain focus on your goal.
3. The major causes of failure and how to change your attitude towards it.

9

MAINTAIN SOUND HEALTH

You want to get the greatest vigour and fullest use from your body. You can do this if you understand two important points:

1. Your body and mind are one, effectively a mind-body.
2. Your mind-body is, in turn, at one with nature.

The health of your mind and body cannot be separated. Anything that affects the soundness of your mind will affect your body, and anything that affects your body will touch your mind. This is why I refer to you as a mind-body.

But you are also affected by your environment, subject to natural laws that govern your mind-body just as much as they affect trees, mountains, birds and beasts.

Understanding the way in which you can maintain a sound mind-body depends, therefore, on understanding the way nature works. You must learn to work with natural forces, not fight them.

THE RHYTHMS OF LIFE

When you consider the waves of the ocean, the passing of the seasons, the waxing and waning of the moon, you will see that nature moves in rhythms. There is even a rhythm in your own life from birth through childhood and adolescence to full maturity, old age and finally birth of a new generation. Light, energy and matter are made up of waves, either moving out in their own rhythm or bound, like a neutron, around the fixed point of the nucleus of the atom.

Nothing about life is static. Movement is constant and rhythmic (though sometimes that rhythm is too large or small for us to perceive immediately). This is one reason why we enjoy music, for it reflects the rhythms and waves of our experience. You must learn to bend and sway with the rhythms of life, not to stand fixed and immobile against them. A sandy beach moves and changes with the rhythms of the waves and lasts for eons; a breakwater is soon destroyed.

Take a look at your life. Is it rhythmical? Are you following work with play, mental effort with physical effort, eating with fasting, seriousness with humour, sex with transmutation of sex into creative effort?

Your subconscious does its best work on your behalf while your conscious mind is at rest. True inspiration most often comes after your subconscious has been given a task and while your conscious mind is then occupied elsewhere—that is, while your mind is playing.

Archimedes had struggled with the complex problem of determining the relative mass of two objects without finding a solution. It was only when he decided to relax and slip into his bath that his subconscious was stimulated by the water he displaced in his tub. He sprang from his bath with that now-famous cry of 'Eureka!' and the solution he had been seeking. Are you giving your mind a chance to relax by playing? Interference with normal rhythmical patterns produces so many problems. If you don't give your mind a rhythm of work and relaxation, your body will be so constantly stimulated that you will likely end up with a stress-related disorder. And without highs and lows, the things that you value begin to pale. Your past failures are what makes success sweet.

You don't really want continuous happiness, for then your happiness would seem dull.

One of the major goals of marriage counselling is getting couples to understand that there is no such thing as being constantly in love. People in love have a series of loves, like waves on the oceans. In the troughs they are neutral in their feelings, but troughs make the peaks of the waves so much more poignant. As in life, not all the ocean's waves are of the same intensity; there are a few for each of us that reach great heights, and it is the memory and exhilaration of these moments that we store up to call upon when the going gets difficult. You have to learn to understand the waves and rhythms in your life and to live within those rhythms in order to be in harmony with the world.

THE INFLUENCE OF YOUR MIND

Just as you have to understand nature as a complex whole, moving with its own rhythms, you have to understand that your mind and body are a whole, each influencing the other.

Humans are the only thinking creatures and this power allows you to modify your world and to learn its laws. You need only to conceive the idea and believe in it to achieve the idea.

This is the story of all the successful people who have changed the path of civilization. It took countless hundreds of millions of years for evolution to develop from all the animals that walked or swam a bird that could fly. Yet the Wright brothers, with childlike faith in their own idea, had human beings airborne in a mere twenty years. That is the power of the mind, demonstrated to us by experience and reinforced by the words of countless prophets in touch with Infinite Intelligence. Christ himself said, 'All things are possible even unto the end of the world.'

Your mind has the higher function in your mind-body. Your body is an exquisitely functioning machine for carrying your mind about and executing the dictates of this powerhouse. A smoothly functioning mind is necessary to a smoothly functioning body.

Some people have bodies that are limited. They can move, see or speak only with difficulty or not at all. Yet the power of their minds allows them to live full creative lives. Helen Keller is a marvellous example, as are Beethoven and Edison, both of whom suffered from severely impaired hearing. Franklin Roosevelt was barely able to stand on his own, yet he inspired and led our country through the greatest depression and war we ever faced. Senator Bob Dole's arm was permanently injured in World War II, but that has not stopped him from becoming one of our most influential political leaders.

The story of civilization is punctuated with greatness achieved by individuals in spite of physical limitations because these people possessed smoothly functioning minds. On the wings of a definite major purpose, faith, enthusiasm and a positive mental attitude, they rose farther and farther from any despair over their limitations toward great heights of brilliant achievement. That is the influence of the mind.

ESSENTIALS OF SUCCESS AND HAPPINESS

Many of the essential principles of success are also essential to a smoothly functioning mind. A definite major purpose and a plan for carrying it out keep you from vacillating in your efforts. Think of a situation in which you were part of a smoothly functioning plan. You were content with the way the situation was handled. You felt at ease and comfortable. Your mind is always satisfied with the harmony produced by a well-organized plan. Anxiety develops from a poorly organized plan.

Controlled attention, self-discipline, accurate thinking, personal initiative, learning from defeat and going the extra mile all are mental tools you can use to organize and carry out your plan. They give you satisfaction both in the achievement of each step of your plan and in your overall progress. Satisfactions are important foods for a healthy mind.

Probably the most important single quality for sound mental health is a positive mental attitude and all that it entails. Two of the greatest destructive forces in the human mind are fear and its close partner, anxiety. They kill enthusiasm, destroy faith, blind vision, blunt creative effort, dispel harmony and peace of mind—all qualities necessary for a positive mental attitude and sound mental health.

THE FORCE OF FEAR

Fear and anxiety produce inharmonious, irritated restlessness in your mind that leads to serious mental maladjustment and produces its counterpart in the body in the form of serious disease, perhaps even death. There is a growing awareness in the healing professions that many human ailments are either the product of mental distress or greatly exacerbated by it.

The list of diseases that are brought on by stress is long, varied, and growing: allergies, asthma, skin disease, hypertension, cardiac problems, arthritis, colitis and immune disorders.

Some hay fever sufferers start sneezing and itching at the

sight of goldenrod in a vase. Tell them the plant is artificial, and their symptoms clear. This is a simple example of how the mind can affect the body negatively.

You must replace fear with understanding and faith in yourself. To do this, let's look at how fear affects the mechanisms of your body.

Temporary, fleeting fear is a normal and important function. It gets you to move out of the way of an oncoming train or keeps you from walking too near a cliff by momentarily focusing your attention—your mind—on a problem. Once the problem is over, this kind of fear is forgotten.

Fear also focuses your bodily functions on a threat. That old story of a cave dweller frightened by a sound in the night is a good illustration. Instantaneously the heart begins pumping faster; blood is diverted from the digestion for use by the muscles; the blood vessels serving the muscles dilate to handle increased volume, while those near the skin contract so that less blood is lost in case of a cut. Hearing becomes more acute; the pupils dilate to take in more light; the adrenaline gland unleashes a torrent of stimulant to provide strength for a fight.

All this is preparation for surviving a battle or chase. The ensuing battle uses up the adrenaline and exhausts the other bodily systems so that they step down from their heightened readiness. Blood leaves the muscles to return to digestive and other functions.

This is an extremely powerful response, one that kept our species alive over millions of years. But it is not intended to be a constant state, for it diverts the body from its normal functions. Still, some of us activate this response to some extent daily or even continually because we live in frequent fear.

You must work to eliminate the causes of those fears.

The fear of the loss of money: have you set up a system to conserve and develop your assets?

The fear of ill health: have you sought and followed worthwhile counsel?

The fear of loss of love: have you put as much effort into increasing your beloved's affection as you would into cultivating an important business prospect?

The fear of death: have you sought help and understanding to the point where fear is replaced by faith?

The list of fears is endless, yet to cultivate a positive mental attitude and develop a smoothly functioning mind that can live in harmony with itself and the world, you must conquer fear and anxiety.

If the same fears and anxieties recur in your mind constantly and are paralysing your efforts, seek the help of a good professional counsellor. You aren't admitting weakness by doing this; you are expressing maturity and commitment to your health and your definite major purpose. A brief period of therapy may mean years of happiness.

Remember that whatever your mind can conceive and believe, it can achieve. Isn't the person who is afraid of falling on the ice the one who falls? Repeating a fear over and over in your mind makes you more susceptible to the things you fear. You must vanquish fear before it vanquishes you.

THE FORCE OF A POSITIVE MENTAL ATTITUDE

The best way to remove fear from your mind is to replace it with PMA.

Émile Coué, the French psychologist, gave us a very simple but practical formula for building PMA and maintaining a health consciousness, 'Every day, in every way, I am getting better and better.' Repeat this sentence to yourself many times a day until your subconscious picks it up, accepts it and begins to carry it out in the form of good health.

This is a simple yet astounding form of autosuggestion. It depends on your belief in the statement, but the best way to build that belief is to make the statement a part of your mental environment. Remember that your mind is strongly influenced by its environment, and by filling that environment with the right thoughts, you will come to believe them.

EATING HABITS

The purpose of food is to supply the body with the things it needs to maintain itself in good repair. Your eating habits must be guided by this goal alone.

Think of your digestive system as a factory. To function efficiently, it has to have a supply of a variety of materials in varying quantities. If you provide the wrong mix of materials, some jobs will never be completed, some will be done with jerry-rigged parts and some materials will simply be stored up in every corner until the walls of the factory begin to swell. Finally, the walls burst, the roof caves in and the factory is either out of business or in need of serious and expensive repair.

Information about nutritional requirements continues to evolve as scientists work to understand more and more about the body. Pay attention to new information (but do not be swept along by fads) as it becomes available. In the main, however, some simple points will keep your diet balanced:

1. Fresh fruits and vegetables should make up the largest portion of your meals. They supply complex mixes of vitamins and trace elements, and your body is designed to avail itself of them easily.

2. Complex carbohydrates, such as breads, grains and potatoes, should be the next largest.
3. Protein, in the form of lean meats, fish and dairy products, is important, but it should not be the centre of your meals. Select small amounts of foods you enjoy, rather than gorge yourself on steak at every meal.
4. Avoid fats; limit your intake of butter and oils, and stay away from deep-fried foods. Also avoid sugars, like candy and colas, which provide little but calories.

Seek variety as well. Your body's nutritional needs run a wide gamut, and the best way to serve those needs without becoming a food chemist is to be sure that you eat a wide spectrum of foods. Don't say, 'I can't eat that way,' for all you are really saying is, 'I don't want to eat that way.' It is a very glib bit of mental gymnastics to make yourself believe that it is impossible to do what is really only unappealing or different. Why should all your efforts for success stumble over your ill health because you don't like broccoli?

Never eat while angry, frightened or worried. Your body is simply not in a position to make use of the food when it is on a defensive footing. Worse, you can make eating a habitual response to stress, which can lead to overweight.

Moderation in food and alcohol intake is important, both because your body can be overwhelmed by an excess of either and because overindulgence can become a trick to avoid dealing with some problem that urgently needs to be faced. If you find that you cannot control either, seek the help of professionals or a worthy organization like Alcoholics or Overeaters Anonymous.

RHYTHMS IN RELAXATION

Relaxation entails completely forgetting the worries and problems of the day. As desirable as this may seem, many people have trouble relaxing.

Your conscious mind selects objects on which to concentrate, and this concentration means the exclusion of other thoughts. You cannot just collapse into a chair and announce, 'I am relaxing', because your mind will select some object of focus, most often the very item you wish to forget about for a time. You need to select an object of relaxation for your mind to concentrate on. It can be kite flying, gardening, reading a novel or anything else which will absorb you.

Television and the corner bar are not the answers. Cultivate a variety of interests that take your mind to new places. Practicing controlled meditation will do wonders for your mental powers. Physical activity can be a terrific thing to immerse yourself in; not only do you relax your mind, but you strengthen your body.

Short periods of relaxation throughout the day can break tension and give your subconscious a chance to work. Read a magazine article; listen to a language tape; work on a crossword puzzle. This is not wasting time; it is keeping your mind in top condition through relaxation.

SLEEP

Your body needs time to rebuild and revitalize itself for the next day. It is sheer stupidity to try to increase your productivity by cutting your sleeping time. Six to eight hours a night are all you need. And remember that even while you sleep, your subconscious is working.

Insomnia is often caused by a failure to relax before going

to bed. Don't work until you drop. Instead wind down at the end of the day by doing something you enjoy that doesn't overstimulate you. (For this reason, exercise is not good just before you go to bed.) Perhaps quiet small talk with your spouse is all you need, or an easy routine of brushing your teeth, stretching for a few moments, or making your bed. A habit which signals your body that it is time for sleep is a valuable aid.

EXERCISE

Ideally your relaxation and play will include exercise. Relaxing and playing are important to your mind, while exercise, which is mostly beneficial to your body, can also be of great mental benefit.

You need to engage in aerobic exercise for a period of twenty minutes at least three times a week to keep your heart and lungs strong. The rate at which you exercise must be determined by your age and physical condition; trainers at any local gym or YMCA can explain this to you and help you design a simple exercise regimen that is neither expensive nor time-consuming. (How much time do you spend watching TV?) Consult your doctor before you begin any exercise program.

Exercise can be a tremendous mental and physical stimulant, clearing away sluggishness. It also teaches you persistence and concentration. Athletic training has become an important field for understanding human potential and has resulted in many techniques that can be applied to your quest for success.

Bill Bowerman was a first-class track coach at the University of Oregon for many years; when he conceived an idea for a better running shoe, the lessons he had learned in training himself and others were an important part of making Nike the number one American shoe manufacturer.

SEX AND SUBLIMATION

Sex is your most precious and constructive drive; it is also the most easily debased. Sex is behind all the creative forces that advance human destiny. Sex has built cathedrals, universities and nations. Why? Because the desire for sex causes us to work to please others, and out of that work spring kindness and the understanding of others.

Sex is a completely natural desire. Do not fear or deny it. But realize that you must direct it, like all desires, to definite ends instead of letting it become an end in itself. If sex is all you want, you will do anything to get it, forgetting your faith in yourself, your definite purpose and your moral standards.

When you want sex, remember that you cannot get something for nothing. The intimacy of sex is gained by constructive work at building a committed relationship. If you channel your desire for sex into creating and providing for that relationship, you will not only get what your heart desires but also attain the heights of achievement.

To work to your greatest good, sex and sublimation need to be alternated in a rhythmical pattern, just as work and play do.

EFFECTIVE MIND-BODY STIMULANTS

At any given time your mind-body may need a boost. Many of the best boosters are things you are already doing; you just need to be conscious of the effect they have and seek them out.

- Sexual expression or a sublimated sexual drive keys up the mind so that it works rapidly and well with real inspiration.
- Love, the ultimate aim of sexual desire, serves a similar purpose; when the two are combined, they are unbeatable.

- Fanning your burning obsession is a strong stimulant.
- Work is a wonderful opportunity for creative expression. Do something small and definite, yet satisfying, like making a phone call or writing a thank-you note.
- A burst of exercise releases pent-up energy, drives away frustration, and stimulates the brain with increased blood and oxygen.
- A little play lets the subconscious go to work.
- Music is full of rhythms, beats and pulses. You can select it to boost your enthusiasm or help you calm down.
- Friendship is a great stimulant. Talk your problems over with others. Laugh with them.
- Your children can inspire you. Build a strong relationship with them, and never neglect to spend as much time with them as possible. Teach your children a skill and renew your self-confidence. Let your children talk to you, and renew your faith.
- Mastermind alliances are powerful stimulants. Seek out the enthusiasm and experience of other people when you need a boost. Mutual suffering causes people to pool their mind power and direct it to relieve that suffering.
- Autosuggestion implants the ideas you want in your mind. Use it whenever you need it.
- Faith and religion are stimulants of the noblest order. Turn to the assurances they offer you and renew your sense of purpose.

Your mental and physical health is inseparable. You cannot work to strengthen one without having a positive effect on the other. Your mind and your body are the navigator and the ship which carry you to the success you desire. Do everything you can to preserve, protect and defend them.

POINTS TO REMEMBER

1. Your mind and body are one.
2. Two of the greatest destructive forces in the human mind are fear and anxiety.
3. Your past failures are what makes success sweet.

10

PEACE OF MIND AND POWER OF MIND

Since what you achieve in life depends on what you first conceive, and this depends first of all upon your deep, inner, subconsciously founded belief— you see that your life depends upon your power to believe.

No, your mere life-processes do not depend upon this power. The Eternal has made it possible for the supreme achievement of evolution, man, to stay alive even without knowing he is alive. The beating of the heart, the pumping of the lungs, the processes of digestion and other vital functions are taken care of by a part of the brain which takes care of itself.

Beyond this, man creates an ever-better species. He aspires—and climbs to the heights of his aspiration. Seeing heights yet beyond, again he aspires—and achieves that peak, beyond which lies another and another.

Significantly, philosophers always have recognized the power of the quiet mind, the peaceful mind. This is far from being a mind empty of aspiration. It is, rather, a mind which can hold, judge and evaluate the highest forms of aspiration. Nor is a peaceful mind the exclusive property of a person who does not move about in the world and busy himself with the world's manifold affairs, for some of the most peaceful minds are the busiest. Remember, we speak of inner peace, like a quiet centre about which all else revolves, like a great rotating dynamo doing useful work and filled with energy, yet referring its rotation always to the unmoved pivot at its middle.

A mind at peace is a mind that is free to conceive greatly. It bears no great conflict within its subconscious which may hamper the conscious mind and therefore conscious action. A mind at peace is a free mind. Its power is limitless.

POINTS TO REMEMBER

1. Your life depends on your power to believe.
2. The power that lies behind a quiet and peaceful mind.
3. A mind at peace is a mind that is free to conceive greatly.

11

THE 17 PRINCIPLES OF SUCCESS

The list that follows is meant to serve as a reminder. Look it over once a week. Are you making regular progress in each of these areas? If you routinely evaluate your efforts to embrace the principles, you are less likely to be caught in a crisis because you've neglected to think accurately, for instance, or to find that your co-workers suddenly regard you as an opportunistic shark.

1. Develop definiteness of purpose
2. Establish a mastermind alliance
3. Assemble an attractive personality
4. Use applied faith
5. Go the extra mile
6. Create personal initiative
7. Build a positive mental attitude
8. Control your enthusiasm
9. Enforce self-discipline
10. Think accurately
11. Control your attention
12. Inspire teamwork
13. Learn from adversity and defeat
14. Cultivate creative vision
15. Maintain sound health

16. Budget your time and money
17. Use cosmic habitforce

A DETAILED EVALUATION

Following are concise summaries of the steps to making each principle a part of your life. Read them through and then use the lines provided at the end of each section to write down specific actions you plan to take to implement the principles.

The summaries themselves will give you concrete recommendations about what to do. Under the definiteness of purpose you might write down that you will define your major goal, write out a plan for achieving it, and read that plan aloud to yourself every day, all of which are mentioned in the summary. But if you also include a date by which you will have your plan written down, you will be making a commitment to yourself that will provide you with extra motivation. So do not simply parrot back the summary's suggestions; consider carefully the changes you need to make and be as detailed as possible in writing them out. In a few weeks or months you can look at these notes, recognize the progress you've made, and renew your commitment to success.

1. Develop DEFINITENESS OF PURPOSE— with PMA
The Starting Point of All Worthwhile Achievements:

You should have one high, desirable, outstanding goal and keep it ever before you. You can have many nonconflicting goals which help you to reach your major definite goal. It is advisable to have immediate, intermediate and distant objectives. When you set a definite major goal, you are apt to recognize that which will help you achieve it.

Determine or fix in your mind exactly what you desire.

Be definite.

Evaluate and determine exactly what you will give in return.

Set a definite date for exactly when you intend to possess your desire.

Identify your desire with a definite plan for carrying out and achieving your objective. Put your plan into action at once.

Clearly define your plan for achievement. Write out precisely and concisely exactly what you want, exactly when you want to achieve it and exactly what you intend to give in return.

Each and every day, morning and evening, read your written statement aloud. As you read it, see, feel and believe yourself already in possession of your objective.

Engage in personal inspection with regularity to determine whether you are on the right track and headed in the right direction so that you don't deviate from the path that leads to the achievement of your objective.

To guarantee success, engage daily in study, thinking and planning time with PMA regarding yourself and your family and how you can achieve your definite goals.

WHATEVER YOUR MIND CAN CONCEIVE AND BELIEVE, YOU CAN ACHIEVE—WHEN YOU HAVE PMA AND APPLY IT.

My commitment to use this principle in my life is:

_____
_____
_____
_____

2. Establish A Mastermind Alliance—with PMA

A mastermind alliance is two or more minds working together in the spirit of perfect harmony toward the attainment of a specific objective.

This principle makes it possible for you, through association with others, to acquire and utilize the knowledge and experience needed for the attainment of any desired goal in

Your mastermind alliance can be created by surrounding yourself or aligning yourself with the advice, counsel and personal cooperation of several people who are willing to lend you their wholehearted aid for the attainment of your objective in the spirit of perfect harmony.

You can create a mastermind alliance with your spouse, your manager, a friend, a co-worker, etc. Once a mastermind alliance is formed, the group as a whole must become and remain active. The group must move in a definite plan, at a definite time, toward a definite common objective. Indecision, inactivity, or delay will destroy usefulness of the alliance. There must be a complete meeting of the minds without reservations on the part of any member.

You can have several mastermind alliances, each with different objectives—i.e., an alliance with your spouse to reach your family objectives, an alliance with your banker or investment counsellor or attorney for your financial objectives, an alliance with your minister or clergy for your spiritual objectives, etc.

My commitment to use this principle in my life is:

_____
_____
_____
_____

3. Assemble an ATTRACTIVE PERSONALITY—with PMA

Your personality is your greatest asset or greatest liability, for it embraces everything that you control: mind, body and soul. A person's personality is the person. It shapes the nature of your thoughts, your deeds, your relationships with others and it establishes the boundaries of the space you occupy in the world.

It is essential that you develop a pleasing personality—pleasing to yourself and to others.

It is imperative that you develop the habit of being sensitive to your own reactions to individuals, circumstances and events and to the reactions of individuals and groups to what you say, think or do.

Positive Factors of a Pleasing Personality

A positive mental attitude

Tolerance

Alertness

Common courtesy

A fondness for people

Flexibility

Tactfulness

Personal magnetism

A pleasant tone of voice

Control of facial expressions

Sportsmanship

Sincerity

A sense of humour

Humility of the heart

Smiling

Enthusiasm Control of temper and emotions

Patience

Proper dress

DO UNTO OTHERS AS YOU WOULD HAVE OTHERS DO UNTO YOU.

My commitment to use this principle in my life is:

_____
_____
_____
_____

4. Use APPLIED FAITH—with PMA

Faith is a state of mind through which your aims, desires, plans and purposes may be translated into their physical or financial equivalent.

Applied faith means action—specifically, the habit of applying your faith under any and all circumstances. It is faith in your God, yourself, your fellowman—and the unlimited opportunities available to you.

Faith without action is dead. Faith is the art of believing by doing. It comes as a result of persistent action. Fear and doubt are faith in reverse gear. Faith, in its positive application, is the key which will give one direct communication with Infinite Intelligence.

Applied faith is belief in an objective or purpose backed by unqualified activity. If you want results, try a prayer. When you pray, express your gratitude and thanksgiving for the blessings you already have received; then ask the Good Lord for his help. Affirm the objectives of your desires through prayer each night and morning. Inspire your imagination to see yourself already in possession of them, and act precisely as if you were already in physical possession of them. The possession of anything first takes place mentally by being imagined in the mind's eye.

PRAYER IS YOUR GREATEST POWER!

My commitment to use this principle in my life is:

_____
_____

5. Go the EXTRA MILE—with PMA

Render more and better service for which you are paid, and do it with a positive mental attitude. Form the habit of going the extra mile because of the pleasure you get out of it and because of what it does to you and for you deep down inside. It is inevitable that every seed of useful service you sow will multiply itself and come back to you in overwhelming abundance.

Following this principle will make you indispensable to other people. The principle manifests itself in two important laws: the Law of Compensation and the Law of Increasing Returns. These unvarying laws always reward intelligent effort rendered in the attitude of faith and rendered instinctively without regards to the limits of immediate compensation.

$$Q1 + Q2 + MA = C$$

The quality of the service rendered plus the quantity of the service rendered plus the mental attitude in which it is rendered equals your compensation in the world and the amount of space you will occupy in the hearts of your fellow man.

MAKE GOING THE EXTRA MILE WITH PMA A HABIT!

My commitment to use this principle in my life is:

_____
_____
_____

6. Create PERSONAL INITIATIVE—with PMA

Personal initiative is the inner power that starts all action. It is the power that inspires the completion of that which one begins. It is the dynamo that starts the faculty of the imagination into action.

It is, in fact, self-motivation.

Motivation is that which induces action or determines choice. It is that which provides a motive. A motive is that inner urge only within the individual which incites you to action, such as an idea, an emotion, a desire or an impulse. It is a hope or other force which starts in an attempt to produce specific results.

When you know principles that can motivate you, you will then know principles that can motivate others.

Motivate yourself with PMA. Hope is the magic ingredient in motivation, but the secret of accomplishment is getting into action.

USE AND DEVELOP THE SELF-STARTER. DO IT NOW!

My commitment to use this principle in my life is:

_____
_____
_____
_____

7. Build a POSITIVE MENTAL ATTITUDE

PMA stands for 'positive mental attitude'.

A positive mental attitude is the right, honest, constructive thought, action or reaction to any person, situation or set of circumstances that does not violate the laws of God or the right of one's fellowman.

PMA allows you to build on hope and overcome the negative attitudes of despair and discouragement. It gives you the mental power, the feeling, the confidence to do anything you make up your mind to do. PMA is commonly referred to as the 'I can...I will' attitude applicable to all challenging circumstances in your life.

You create and maintain a positive mental attitude through your own willpower, based on motives of your own adaption. To develop PMA, strive to understand and apply the Golden Rule; be considerate and sensitive to the reactions of others; be sensitive to your own reactions by controlling your emotional responses; be a good finder; believe that any goal can be achieved; and develop what are understood to be right habits of thought and action.

A positive mental attitude is the catalyst necessary for achieving worthwhile success. Achievement is attained through some combination of PMA and definiteness of purpose with one or more of the other fifteen success principles.

MAINTAIN THE RIGHT ATTITUDE—A POSITIVE MENTAL ATTITUDE.

My commitment to use this principle in my life is:

_____
_____
_____
_____

8. Control Your Enthusiasm—with PMA

A person without enthusiasm is like a watch without a mainspring. Father John O'Brien, research professor of theology at the University of Notre Dame, says, 'the first ingredient which I believe is absolutely necessary for a successful, efficient and competent individual is enthusiasm.' He adds, 'Enthusiasm comes from the Greek words that let you look into the root of this word—into its basic, fundamental and original meaning. The first is *theos*, which means God. The other two words are *en-Tae*, so that in the early usage of this term of the ancient Greeks, it literally meant, "God within you."' Further, 'No battle of any importance can be won without enthusiasm.'

To become enthusiastic about achieving a desirable goal, keep your mind on that goal day after day. The more worthy and desirable your objectives, the more dedicated and enthusiastic you will become. Understand and act on William James's statement, 'The emotions are not always immediately subject to reason but they are always immediately subject to ACTION' (emphasis added). Enthusiasm thrives on a positive mind and positive action. This is the key to controlling your enthusiasm: always give it a worthy goal to focus on and once you have channelled it toward that goal, it will carry you forward.

Real enthusiasm comes from within. However, enthusiasm is like getting water from a well; first you have to prime the pump but soon the water flows and flows and flows. You can be enthusiastic about everything and anything you know or do. Enthusiasm is a PMA characteristic. It can be generated naturally from one's thoughts, feelings and emotions, but more important, it can be generated at will.

TO BE ENTHUSIASTIC… ACT ENTHUSIASTICALLY!

My commitment to use the principle in my life is:

_____
_____
_____
_____

9. Enforce SELF-DISCIPLINE—with PMA

Self-discipline enables you to develop control over yourself. Self-discipline begins with mastery of your thoughts, what you really are, what you really do. Your failures and your successes are the results of habits. We are creatures of habit, but because we are minds with bodies, we can change our habits.

Self-discipline is perhaps the most important function in aiding an individual in the development and maintenance of habits of thought which enable that person to fix his or her entire attention upon any desired purpose and to hold it there until that purpose has been attained.

If you do not control your thoughts, you do not control your deeds. Think first and act afterward. Self-discipline is the principle by which you may voluntarily shape the patterns of your thoughts to harmonize with your goals and purposes.

DIRECT YOUR THOUGHTS, CONTROL YOUR EMOTIONS, ORDAIN YOUR DESTINY WITH PMA.

My commitment to use this principle in my life is:

_____
_____
_____
_____

10. THINK ACCURATELY—with PMA

Accurate thinking is b2ased on two major fundamentals:

1. Inductive reasoning, based on the assumption of unknown facts or hypotheses.
2. Deductive reasoning, based on known facts or what are believed to be facts.

In school we are taught deductive and inductive reasoning and the fallacy that results in starting with the wrong premise in the one instance and making the wrong inference in the other. Accurate thinking and common sense are in part the result of experiences. You can learn from your own experiences as well as those of others when you learn how to recognize, relate, assimilate and apply principles in order to achieve your goals.

1. Separate facts from fiction or hearsay evidence.
2. Separate facts into classes: important and unimportant.

Be careful of others' opinions. They could be dangerous and destructive. Make sure your opinions are not someone else's prejudices. The accurate thinker learns to use his or her own judgment and to be cautious no matter who may endeavour to influence him or her.

TRUTH WILL BE TRUTH REGARDLESS OF A CLOSED MIND, IGNORANCE OR REFUSAL TO BELIEVE.

My commitment to use this principle in my life is:

_____
_____
_____
_____

11. Control YOUR ATTENTION—with PMA

Controlled attention is organized mind power. It is the highest form of self-discipline. Controlled attention is the act of coordinating all the faculties of the mind and directing their combined power to a given end or definite objective. It is an act that can be obtained only by the strictest sort of self-discipline.

It is obvious, therefore, that when you voluntarily fix your attention upon a definite major purpose of a positive nature and force your mind through your daily habits of thought to dwell on the subject, you condition your subconscious mind to act on that purpose. Controlled attention, when it is focused upon the object of your definite major purpose, is a medium by which you make positive application of the principle of suggestion.

The mind never remains inactive, not even during sleep. It works continuously by reactions to the influences which reach it. Therefore, the object of controlled attention is that of keeping your mind busy with thought material which may be helpful in attaining the object of your desire.

Controlled attention is self-mastery of the highest order, for it is an accepted fact that the person who controls his or her own mind may control everything else.

KEEP YOUR MIND ON THE THINGS YOU WANT AND OFF THE THINGS YOU DON'T WANT.

My commitment to use this principle in my life is:

_____
_____
_____
_____

12. Inspire TEAMWORK—with PMA

Teamwork is a willing cooperation and the coordination of effort to achieve a specific objective. When the spirit of teamwork is willing, voluntary and free, it leads to the attainment of great and enduring power.

It is a system which coordinates all the team players' resources and talents and automatically discourages dishonesty and unfairness, while it adequately compensates the individuals who serve honestly and unselfishly.

The principle of teamwork differs from the mastermind principle in that it is based on the coordination of effort without necessarily embracing the principle of definiteness of purpose or the principle of harmony, two important essentials of the mastermind.

Teamwork produces power, but the question of whether the power is temporary or permanent depends on the motive that inspired the cooperation. If the motive is one that inspires people to cooperate willingly, the power produced by this sort of teamwork will endure as long as that spirit of willingness prevails.

Teamwork builds individuals and businesses and provides unlimited opportunity for all. It is sharing a part of what you have—a part that is good—with others.

THAT WHICH YOU SHARE WILL MULTIPLY;
THAT WHICH YOU WITHHOLD WILL DIMINISH.

My commitment to use this principle in my life is:

_____
_____
_____
_____

13. Learn from ADVERSITY AND DEFEAT—with PMA

Every adversity carries with it the seed of an equivalent or greater benefit for those who have PMA and apply it.

Defeat may be a stepping-stone or a stumbling block, according to your mental attitude and how you relate it to yourself.

It is never the same as failure unless and until it has been accepted as such.

Your mental attitude in respect to defeat is the factor of major importance which determines whether you ride with tides of fortune or misfortune. The person with a positive metal attitude reacts to defeat in the spirit of determination not to accept it. The person with a negative mental attitude reacts to defeat in the spirit of hopeless acceptance.

THE WORST THING THAT HAPPENS TO YOU MAY BE THE BEST THING THAT CAN HAPPEN TO YOU IF YOU DON'T LET IT GET THE BEST OF YOU.

My commitment to use this principle in my life is:

_____
_____

14. Cultivate CREATIVE VISION—with PMA

Man's greatest gift is his thinking mind. It analyses, compares, chooses. It creates, visualizes, foresees and generates ideas.

Imagination is your mind's exercise, challenge and adventure. It is the key to all of a person's achievements, the mainspring of all human endeavour, the secret door to the soul of a person. Imagination inspires human endeavour in connection with material things and ideas associated with material things.

Imagination is the workshop of the human mind, where old ideas and established facts may be assembled into new combinations and put to new uses. It is the act of constructive intellect in the grouping of materials, knowledge or thoughts into new, original and rational systems, a constructive or creative faculty embracing poetic, artistic, philosophical, scientific and ethical imagination.

Creative vision may be an inborn quality of the mind or an acquired quality, for it may be developed by the free and fearless use of the faculty of imagination.

Creative vision extends beyond interest in material things. It judges the future by the past and concerns itself with the future more than with the past. Imagination is influenced and controlled by the powers of reason and experience. Creative vision pushes these aside and attains its ends by basically new ideas and methods.

One of the ways to increase your flow of ideas is by developing the habit of taking study time, thinking time and planning time. Be quiet and motionless, and listen for that small, still voice that speaks from within as you contemplate the ways in which you can achieve your objectives.

WHAT CAN BE CONCEIVED CAN BE CREATED—WITH PMA.

My commitment to use this principle in my life is:

_____
_____
_____
_____

15. Maintain SOUND HEALTH—with PMA

You are a mind with a body. Inasmuch as your brain controls your body, recognize that sound physical health demands a positive mental attitude, a health consciousness. Establish good, well-balanced health habits in work, play, rest, nourishment and study. To maintain a health consciousness, think in terms of good physical health, not in terms of illness or disease. Remember, what your mind focuses upon, your mind brings into existence, whether it is financial success or physical health.

To maintain a positive attitude for the development and maintenance of a sound health consciousness, use self-discipline, keep your mind free of negative thoughts and influence and create and maintain a well-balanced life. Follow work with play, mental effort with physical effort, seriousness with humour, and you will be on the road to good health and happiness.

A sound mind and a sound body are attainable if you will put PMA to work for you. Remember, you can enjoy good health and live longer with PMA.

I FEEL HEALTHY! I FEEL HAPPY! I FEEL TERRIFIC!

My commitment to use this principle in my life is:

_____
_____
_____
_____

16. Budget your TIME AND MONEY—with PMA

Intelligently balance your use of time and resources, both business and personal. Take inventory of yourself and your activities so that you discover where and how you are spending your time and your money.

Engage in study, thinking and planning time.

Don't waste your time or your money. 10 per cent of all you earn is yours to keep and invest. Like any good business, budget your money. Use your time wisely toward attainment of your objectives. Develop a plan for the use of your income for expenses, savings and investments.

YOU DON'T ALWAYS GET WHAT YOU EXPECT UNLESS YOU INSPECT—WITH PMA.

My commitment to use this principle in my life is:

_____
_____
_____
_____

17. Use cosmic HABITFORCE—with PMA

Cosmic habitforce pertains to the entire universe and is the law by which the equilibrium of the universe is maintained through established patterns or habits. It is the law which forces every living creature and every particle of matter to come under the dominating influence of its environment, including the physical habits and thought habits of humankind.

Cosmic habitforces are the powers which you apply with PMA when you use the universal laws or principles. Cosmic habitforces are employed when you use your mind powers whether they pertain to your conscious or subconscious mind. That is how you think and grow richer or achieve anything in life you desire (in principle) that doesn't violate the laws of God or the rights of your fellowman.

All of us are ruled by habits. These are fastened upon us by repeated thoughts and experiences. You have complete right of control over your thoughts. We create patterns of thought by repeating certain ideas or behaviour until the Law of Cosmic Habitforce takes over those patterns and makes them more or less permanent unless or until you consciously rearrange them.

Habits: you have them—some good, perhaps others bad. Many you are aware of, but some that are undesirable you are blinded to. Each begins in your mind consciously or subconsciously. And each can be developed and neutralized or changed at will through the proper use of your mind. You have this power.

You are ruled by your habits. It takes a habit to replace a habit. Develop positive habits that will be in harmony with the achievement of your definite purpose or goal.

> SOW AN ACT, AND YOU REAP A HABIT.
> SOW A HABIT, AND YOU REAP A CHARACTER.
> SOW A CHARACTER, AND YOU REAP A DESTINY.

POINTS TO REMEMBER

1. Determine or fix in your mind exactly what you desire. Be definite.
2. Create mastermind alliances.
3. It is essential to develop a pleasing personality.

12

GOLDEN RULE

There is more power wrapped up in the preceding lessons of this course than most men could trust themselves with; therefore, this lesson is a governor that will, if observed and applied, enable you to steer your ship of knowledge over the rocks and reefs of failure that usually beset the pathway of all who come suddenly into possession of power.

For more than twenty-five years I have been observing the manner in which men behave themselves when in possession of power, and I have been forced to the conclusion that the man who attains it in any other than by the slow, step-by-step process, is constantly in danger of destroying himself and all whom he influences.

It must have become obvious to you, long before this, that this entire course leads to the attainment of *power* of proportions which may be made to perform the seemingly 'impossible'. Happily, it becomes apparent that this power can only be attained by the observance of many fundamental principles all of which converge in this lesson, which is based upon a law that both equals and transcends in importance every other law outlined in the preceding lessons.

Likewise, it becomes apparent to the thoughtful student that this *power* can endure only by faithful observance of the law upon which this lesson is based, wherein lies the 'safety-valve' that protects the careless student from the dangers of his own follies; and protects, also, those whom he might endanger if he tried to circumvent the injunction laid down in this lesson.

To 'prank' with the power that may be attained from the knowledge wrapped up in the preceding lessons of this course, without a full understanding and strict observance of the law laid down in this lesson, is the equivalent of 'pranking' with a power which may destroy as well as create.

I am speaking, now, not of that which I suspect to be true, but, of that which I KNOW TO BE TRUE! The truth upon which this entire course, and this lesson in particular, is founded, is no invention of mine. I lay no claim to it except that of having observed its unvarying application in the everyday walks of life over a period of more than twenty-five years of struggle; and, of having appropriated as much of it as, in the light of my human frailties and weaknesses, I could make use of.

If you demand *positive* proof of the soundness of the laws upon which this course in general, and this lesson in particular, is founded, I must plead inability to offer it except through one witness, and that is *yourself*.

You may have *positive* proof only by testing and applying these laws for yourself.

If you demand more substantial and authoritative evidence than my own, then I am privileged to refer you to the teachings and philosophy of Christ, Plato, Socrates, Epictetus, Confucius, Emerson and two of the more modern philosophers, James and Münsterberg, from whose works I have appropriated all that constitutes the more important fundamentals of this lesson, with the exception of that which I have gathered from my own limited experience.

For more than four thousand years men have been preaching

the Golden Rule as a suitable rule of conduct among men, but unfortunately the world has accepted the letter while totally missing the spirit of this Universal Injunction. We have accepted the Golden Rule philosophy merely as a sound rule of ethical conduct but we have failed to understand the law upon which it is based.

I have heard the Golden Rule quoted scores of times, but I do not recall having ever heard an explanation of the law upon which it is based, and not until recent years did I understand that law, from which I am led to believe that those who quoted it did not understand it.

The Golden Rule means, substantially, to do unto others as you would wish them to do unto you if your positions were reversed.

But why? What is the *real* reason for this kindly consideration of others?

The real reason is this:

There is an eternal law through the operation of which we reap that which we sow. When you select the rule of conduct by which you guide yourself in your transactions with others, you will be fair and just, very likely, if you know that you are setting into motion, by that selection, a *power* that will run its course for weal or woe in the lives of others, returning, finally, to help or to hinder you, according to its nature.

'Whatsoever a man soweth that shall be also reap!'

It is your privilege to deal unjustly with others, but, if you understand the law upon which the Golden Rule is based, you must know that your unjust dealings will 'come home to roost'.

If you fully understood the principles described in Lesson Eleven, on *accurate thought*, it will be quite easy for you to understand the law upon which the Golden Rule is based. You cannot pervert or change the course of this law, *but you can adapt yourself to its nature and thereby use it as an irresistible power that will carry you to heights of achievement which could not be attained without its aid.*

This law does not stop by merely flinging back upon you your acts of injustice and unkindness toward others; it goes further than this—much further—and returns to you the results of every *thought* that you release.

Therefore, not alone is it advisable to 'do unto others as you wish them to do unto you', but to avail yourself fully of the benefits of this great Universal Law you must 'think of others as you wish them to think of you'.

The law upon which the Golden Rule is based begins affecting you, either for good or evil, the moment you release a *thought*. It has amounted almost to a worldwide tragedy that people have not generally understood this law. Despite the simplicity of the law, it is practically all there is to be learned that is of enduring value to man, for it is the medium through which we become the masters of our own destiny.

Understand this law and you understand *all* that the Bible has to unfold to you, for the Bible presents one unbroken chain of evidence in support of the fact that man is the maker of his own destiny; and, that his *thoughts* and *acts* are the tools with which he does the *making*.

During ages of less enlightenment and tolerance than that of the present, some of the greatest thinkers the world has ever produced have paid with their lives for daring to uncover this Universal Law so that it might be understood by all. In the light of the past history of the world, it is an encouraging bit of evidence, in support of the fact that men are gradually throwing off the veil of ignorance and intolerance, to note that I stand in no danger of bodily harm for writing that which would have cost me my life a few centuries ago.

◆

While this course deals with the highest laws of the universe, which man is capable of interpreting, the aim, nevertheless, has been to show how these laws may be used in the practical affairs of life.

THE POWER OF PRAYER

Neither this lesson nor the course of which it is a part is based upon an appeal to maudlin sentiment, but there can be no escape from the truth that *success,* in its highest and noblest form, brings one, finally, to view all human relationships with a feeling of deep emotion such as that which this lawyer felt when he overheard the old man's prayer.

If may be an old-fashioned idea, but somehow I can't get away from the belief that *no man can attain success in its highest form without the aid of earnest prayer!*

Prayer is the key with which one may open the secret doorway. In this age of mundane affairs, when the uppermost thought of the majority of people id centred upon the accumulation of wealth, or the struggle for a mere existence, it is both easy and natural for us to overlook the power of earnest prayer.

I am not saying that you should resort to prayer as a means of solving your daily problems which press for immediate attention; no, I am not going that far in a course of instruction which will be studied largely by those who are seeking in it the road to *success* that is measured in dollars; but, may I not modestly suggest to *you* that you, at least, give *prayer* a trial after *everything else jails* to bring you a *satisfying success?*

The Golden Rule philosophy is based upon a law which no man can circumvent. This law is through the operation of which one's thoughts are transformed into reality corresponding exactly to the nature of the thoughts.

'Once grant the creative power of our thought and there is an end of struggling for our own way, and an end of gaining it *at someone else's expense;* for, since by the terms of the hypothesis we can create what we like, the simplest way of getting what we want is, not to snatch it from somebody else, but to make it for ourselves; and, since there is no limit to thought there can be no need for straining, and for everyone to have his own way in *this manner*, would be to banish all strife, want, sickness and sorrow from the earth.

'Now, it is precisely on this assumption of the creative power of our thought that the whole Bible rests. If not, what is the meaning of being saved by Faith? Faith is essentially thought; and, therefore, every call to have faith in God is a call to trust in the power of our own thought about God. "According to your faith be it unto you," says the Old Testament. The entire book is nothing but one continuous statement of the creative power of Thought.

'The Law of Man's Individuality is, therefore, the Law of Liberty, and equally it is the Gospel of peace; for when we truly understand the law of our own individuality, we see that the same law finds its expression in everyone else; and, consequently, we shall reverence *the law in others* exactly in proportion as we value it in ourselves. To do this is to follow the Golden Rule of doing to others what we would they should do unto us; and because we know that the Law of Liberty in ourselves must include the free use of our creative power, there is no longer any inducement to infringe the rights of others, for we can satisfy all our desires by the exercise of our knowledge of the law.

'As this comes to be understood, co-operation will take the place of competition, with the result of removing all ground for enmity, whether between individuals, classes or nations…'

(The foregoing quotation is from Bible Mystery and Bible Meaning by the late Judge T. Troward, published by Robert McBride & Company, New York City. Judge Troward was the author of several interesting volumes, among them The Edinburgh Lectures, which is recommended to all students of this course.)

If you wish to know what happens to a man when he totally disregards the law upon which the Golden Rule philosophy is based, pick out any man in your community whom you know to live for the single dominating purpose of accumulating wealth and who has no conscientious scruples as to how he accumulates that wealth. Study this man and you will observe that there is no warmth to his soul; there is no kindness to his words; there is no welcome to his face. He has become a slave to the desire for wealth; he is too busy to enjoy life and too selfish to wish to help others enjoy it. He walks, and talks, and breathes, but he is nothing but a human automaton. Yet there are many who envy such a man and wish that they might occupy his position, foolishly believing him to be a *success.*

There can never be *success* without happiness, and no man can be happy without dispensing happiness to others. Moreover, the dispensation must be voluntary and with no other object in view than that of spreading sunshine into the hearts of those whose hearts are heavy-laden with burdens.

George D. Herron had in mind the law upon which the Golden Rule philosophy is based when he said, 'We have talked much of the brotherhood to come; but brotherhood has always been the fact of our life, long before it became a modern and inspired sentiment. Only we have been brothers in slavery and torment, brothers in ignorance and its perdition, brothers in disease, and war, and want, brothers in prostitution and hypocrisy. What happens to one of us sooner or later happens to all; we have always been unescapably involved in common destiny. The world constantly tends to the level of the down most man in it; and that down most man is the world's real ruler, hugging it close to his bosom, dragging it down to his death. You do not think so, but it is true, and it ought to be true. For if there were some way by which some of us could get free, apart from others, if there were some way by which some of us could have heaven while others had hell, if there were some way by which part of the world could escape some form of the blight and peril and misery of disinherited labour, then indeed would our world be lost and damned; but since men have never been able to separate themselves from one another's woes and wrongs, since history is fairly stricken with the lesson that we cannot escape brotherhood of some kind, since the whole of life is teaching us that we are hourly choosing between brotherhood in suffering and brotherhood in good, it remains for us to choose the brotherhood of a co-operative world, with all its fruits thereof—the fruits of *love* and *liberty*.'

LEARN TO LIVE AND LET LIVE

The world war ushered us into an age of co-operative effort in which the law of 'live and let live' stands out like a shining star to guide us in our relationships with each other. This great universal call for co-operative effort is taking on many forms, not the least important of which are the Rotary Clubs, the Kiwanis Clubs, the Lions Clubs and the many other luncheon clubs which bring men together in a spirit of friendly intercourse, for these clubs mark the beginning of an age of friendly competition in business. The next step will be a closer alliance of all such clubs in an out-and-out spirit of friendly cooperation.

The attempt by Woodrow Wilson and his contemporaries to establish the League of Nations, followed by the efforts of Warren G. Harding to give footing to the same cause under the name of the World Court, marked the first attempt in the history of the world to make the Golden Rule effective as a common meeting ground for the nations of the world.

There is no escape from the fact that the world has awakened to the truth in George D. Herron's statement that, 'we are hourly choosing between brotherhood in suffering and brotherhood in good.' The world war has taught us—nay, forced upon us—the truth that a part of the world cannot suffer without injury to the whole world. These facts are called to your attention, not in the nature of a preachment on morality, but for the purpose of directing your attention to the underlying law through which these changes are being brought about. For more than four thousand years the world has been thinking about the Golden Rule philosophy, and that *thought* is now becoming transformed into realization of the benefits that accrue to those who apply it.

Still mindful of the fact that the student of this course is interested in a material success that can be measured by bank balances, it seems appropriate to suggest here that all who will may profit by shaping their business philosophy to conform with this sweeping change toward co-operation which is taking place all over the world.

If you can grasp the significance of the tremendous change that has come over the world since the close of the world war, and if you can interpret the meaning of all the luncheon clubs and other similar gatherings which bring men and women together in a spirit of friendly cooperation, surely your imagination will suggest to you the fact that this is an opportune time to profit by adopting this spirit of friendly co-operation as the basis of your own business or professional philosophy.

Stated conversely, it must be obvious to all who make any pretence of thinking accurately, that the time is at hand when failure to adopt the Golden Rule as the foundation of one's business or professional philosophy is the equivalent of economic suicide.

♦

Perhaps you have wondered why the subject of *honesty* has not been mentioned in this course, as a prerequisite to *success,* and, if so, the answer will be found in this lesson. The Golden Rule philosophy, when rightly understood and applied, makes dishonesty impossible. It does more than this—it makes impossible all the other destructive qualities such as selfishness, greed, envy, bigotry, hatred and malice.

When you apply the Golden Rule, you become, at one and the same time, both the judge and the judged—the accused and the accuser. This places one in a position in which *honesty* begins in one's own heart, toward one's self and extends to all others with equal effect. *Honesty* based upon the Golden Rule is not the brand of honesty which recognizes nothing but the question of expediency.

It is no credit to be honest, when honesty is obviously the most *profitable* policy, lest one lose a good customer or a valuable client or be sent to jail for trickery. But when honesty means either a temporary or a permanent material loss, then it becomes an *honour* of the highest degree to all who practice it. Such honesty has its appropriate reward in the accumulated power of character and reputation enjoyed, by all who deserve it.

Those who understand and apply the Golden Rule philosophy are always scrupulously honest, not alone out of their desire to be just with others, but because of their desire to be just with themselves. They understand the eternal law upon which the Golden Rule is based, and they know that through the operation of this law *every thought thy release and every act in which they indulge has its counterpart in some fact or circumstance with which thy will later be confronted.*

Golden Rule philosophers are honest because they understand the truth that honesty adds to their own character that 'vital something' which gives it life and power. Those who understand the law through which the Golden Rule operates would poison their own drinking water as quickly as they would indulge in acts of injustice to others, for they know that such injustice starts a chain of causation that will not only bring them physical suffering, but will destroy their characters, stain for ill their reputations and render impossible the attainment of enduring success.

The law through which the Golden Rule philosophy operates is none other than the law through which the principle of Autosuggestion operates. This statement gives you a suggestion from which you should be able to make a deduction of a far-reaching nature and of inestimable value.

Test your progress in the mastery of this course by analysing the foregoing statement and determining, before you read on, what suggestion it offers you.

Of what possible benefit could it be to you to know that when you do unto others as if you were the others, which is the sum and substance of the Golden Rule, you are putting into motion a chain of causation through the aid of a law which affects the others according to the nature of your act, *and at the same time planting in your character, through your subconscious mind, the effects of that act.*

This question practically suggests its own answer, but as I am determined to cause you to think this vital subject out for yourself, I will put the question in still another form, viz.:

If all your acts toward others, and even your thoughts of others, are registered in your subconscious mind, through the principle of auto-suggestion, thereby building your own character in exact duplicate of your *thoughts* and *acts,* can you not see how important it is to guard those acts and thoughts?

We are now in the very heart of the real reason for doing unto others as we would have them do unto us, for it is obvious that whatever we do unto others we do unto ourselves.

Stated in another way, every *act* and every *thought* you release modifies your own character in exact conformity with the nature of the act or thought, and your character is a sort of centre of magnetic attraction which attracts to you the people and conditions that harmonize with it.

You cannot indulge in an act toward another person without having first created the nature of that act in your own thought, and you cannot release a thought without planting the sum and substance and nature of it in your own sub-conscious mind, there to become a part and parcel of your own character.

Grasp this simple principle and you will understand why you cannot afford to hate or envy another person. You will also understand why you cannot afford to strike back, in kind, at those who do you an injustice. Likewise, you will understand the injunction, 'Return good for evil.'

Understand the law upon which the Golden Rule injunction is based and you will understand, also, the law that eternally binds all mankind in a single bond of fellowship and renders it impossible for you to injure another person, by *thought ox deed*, without injuring yourself; and, likewise, adds to your own character the results of every kind *thought* and *deed* in which you indulge.

Understand this law and you will then know, beyond room for the slightest doubt, that you are constantly punishing yourself for every wrong you commit and rewarding yourself for every act of constructive conduct in which you indulge.

It seems almost an act of Providence that the greatest wrong and the most severe injustice ever done me by one of my fellow men was done just as I began this lesson. (Some of the students of this course will know what it is to which I refer.)

This injustice has worked a temporary hardship on me, but that is of little consequence compared to the advantage it has given me by providing a timely opportunity for me to test the soundness of the entire premise upon which this lesson is founded.

The injustice to which I refer left two courses of action open to me. I could have claimed relief by 'striking back' at my antagonist, through both civil court action and criminal libel proceedings, or I could have stood upon my right to forgive him. One course of action would have brought me a substantial sum—of money and whatever joy and satisfaction there may be in defeating and *punishing* an enemy. The other course of action would have brought me self-respect which is enjoyed by those who have successfully met the test and discovered that they have evolved to the point at which they can repeat the Lord's Prayer and *mean it!*

I chose the latter course. I did so, despite the recommendations of close personal friends to 'strike back', and despite the offer of a prominent lawyer to do my 'striking' for me *without cost.*

But the lawyer offered to do the impossible, for the reason that no man can 'strike back' at another *without cost.* Not always is the cost of a monetary nature, for there are other things with which one may pay that are dearer than money.

It would be as hopeless to try to make one who was not familiar with the law upon which the Golden Rule is based understand why I refused to strike back at this enemy as it would to try to describe the law of gravitation to an ape. If you understand this law you understand, also, why I chose to *forgive* my enemy.

In the Lord's Prayer we are admonished to forgive our enemies, but that admonition will fall on deaf ears except where the listener understands the law upon which it is based. That law is none other than the law upon which the Golden Rule is based. It is the law that forms the foundation of this entire lesson, and through which we must inevitably reap that which we sow. There is no escape from the operation of this law, nor is there any cause to try to avoid its consequences if we refrain from putting into motion *thoughts* and *acts* that are destructive.

That we may more concretely describe the law upon which this lesson is based, let us embody the law in a code of ethics such as one who wishes to follow literally the injunction of the Golden Rule might appropriately adopt, as follows.

MY CODE OF ETHICS

I. I believe in the Golden Rule as the basis of all human conduct; therefore, I will never do to another person that which I would not be willing for that person to do to me if our positions were reversed.

II. I will be honest, even to the slightest detail, in all my transactions with others, not alone because of my desire to be fair with them, but because of my desire to impress the idea of honesty on my own subconscious mind, thereby weaving this essential quality into my own character.

III. I will forgive those who are unjust toward me, with no thought as to whether they deserve it or not, because I understand the law through which forgiveness of others strengthens my own character and wipes out the effects of my own transgressions, in my subconscious mind.

IV. I will be just, generous and fair with others always, even though I know that these acts will go unnoticed and unrecorded, in the ordinary terms of reward, because I understand and intend to apply the law through the aid of which one's own character is but the sum total of one's own *acts* and *deeds*.

V. Whatever time I may have to devote to the discovery and exposure of the weaknesses and faults of others I will devote, more profitably, to the discovery and *correction* of my own.

VI. I will slander no person, no matter how much I may believe another person may deserve it, because I wish to plant no destructive suggestions in my own sub-conscious mind.

VII. I recognize the power of Thought as being an inlet leading into my brain from the universal ocean of life; therefore, I will set no destructive thoughts afloat upon that ocean lest they pollute the minds of others.

VIII. I will conquer the common human tendency toward hatred, and envy, and selfishness, and jealousy, and malice, and pessimism, and doubt, and fear; for I believe these to be the seed from which the world harvests most of its troubles.

IX. When my mind is not occupied with thoughts that tend toward the attainment of my *definite chief aim* in life, I will voluntarily keep it filled with thoughts of courage, and self- confidence, and goodwill toward others, and faith, and kindness, and loyalty, and love for truth, and justice, for I believe these to be the seed from which the world reaps its harvest of progressive growth.

X. I understand that a mere passive belief in the soundness of the Golden Rule philosophy is of no value whatsoever, either to myself or to others; therefore, I will *actively* put into operation this universal rule for good in all my transactions with others.

XI. I understand the law through the operation of which my own character is developed from my own *acts* and *thoughts*; therefore, I will guard with care all that goes into its development.

XII. Realizing that enduring happiness comes only through helping others find it; that no act of kindness is without its reward, even though it may never be directly repaid, I will do my best to assist others when and where the opportunity appears.

You have noticed frequent reference to Emerson throughout this course. Every student of the course should own a copy of Emerson's Essays, and the essay on Compensation should be read and studied at least every three months. Observe, as you read this essay, that it deals with the same law as that upon which the Golden Rule is based.

There are people who believe that the Golden Rule philosophy is nothing more than a theory, and that it is in no way connected with an immutable law. They have arrived at this conclusion because of personal experience wherein they rendered service to others without enjoying the benefits of direct reciprocation.

How many are there who have not rendered service to others that was neither reciprocated nor appreciated? I am sure that I have had such an experience, not once, but many times, and I am equally sure that I will have similar experiences in the future, nor will I discontinue rendering service to others merely because *they* neither reciprocate nor appreciate my efforts.

And here is the reason:

When I render service to another, or indulge in an act of kindness, I store away in my sub-conscious mind the effect of my efforts, which may be likened to the 'charging' of an electric battery. By and by, if I indulge in a sufficient number of such acts, I will have developed a positive, dynamic character that will *attract* to me people who harmonize with or resemble my own character.

Those whom I *attract* to me will reciprocate the acts of kindness and the service that I have rendered others, thus the Law of Compensation will have balanced the scales of justice for me, bringing back from one source the results of service that I rendered through an entirely different source.

You have often heard it said that a salesman's first sale should be to himself, which means that unless he first convinces himself of the merits of his wares he will not be able to convince others. Here, again, enters this same Law of Attraction, for it is a well-known fact that *enthusiasm* is contagious, and when a salesman shows great *enthusiasm* over his wares, he will arouse a corresponding interest in the minds of others.

You can comprehend this law quite easily by regarding yourself as a sort of human magnet that attracts those whose characters harmonize with your own. In thus regarding yourself as a magnet that attracts to you all who harmonize with your dominating characteristics and repels all who do not so harmonize, you should keep in mind, also, the fact that *you are the builder of that magnet;* also, that you may change its nature so that it will correspond to any ideal that you may wish to set up and follow.

And, most important of all, you should keep in mind the fact that this entire process of change takes place through *thought!*

Your character is but the sum total of your *thoughts* and *deeds!* This truth has been stated in many different ways throughout this course.

Because of this great truth it is impossible for you to render any useful service or indulge in any act of kindness toward others without benefiting thereby. Moreover, it is just as impossible for you to indulge in any destructive *act* or *thought* without paying the penalty in the loss of a corresponding amount of your own power.

◆

Positive thought develops a dynamic personality. *Negative thought* develops a personality of an opposite nature. In many of the preceding lessons of this course, and in this one, definite instructions are given: as to the exact method of developing personality through *positive thought*. These instructions are particularly detailed in Lesson Three, on *Self-confidence*. In that lesson you have a very definite formula to follow. All of the formulas provided in this course are for the purpose of helping you *consciously* to direct the power of *thought* in the development of a personality that will attract to you those who will be of help in the attainment of your *definite chief aim*.

You need no proof that your hostile or unkind *acts* toward others bring back the effects of retaliation. Moreover, this retaliation is usually definite and immediate. Likewise, you need no proof that you can accomplish more by dealing with others in such a way that they will want to co-operate with you. If you mastered the eighth lesson, on Self-control, you now understand how to induce others to act toward you as you wish them to act— *through your own attitude toward them.*

The law of 'an eye for an eye and a tooth for a tooth' is based upon the self-same law as that upon which the Golden

Rule operates. This is nothing more than the law of retaliation with which all of us are familiar. Even the most selfish person will respond to this law, *because he cannot help it!* If I speak ill of you, even though 1 tell the truth, you will not think kindly of me. Furthermore, you will most likely retaliate in kind. But, if I speak of your virtues, you will think kindly of me, and when the opportunity appears you will reciprocate in kind in the majority of instances.

Through the operation of this law of attraction the uninformed are constantly attracting trouble and grief and hatred and opposition from others by their *unguarded words* and *destructive acts*.

Do unto others as you would have them do unto you!

We have heard that injunction expressed thousands of times, yet how many of us understand the law upon which it is based? To make this injunction somewhat clearer it might be well to state it more in detail, about as follows:

Do unto others as you would have them do unto you, *bearing in mind the fact that human nature has a tendency to retaliate in kind.*

Confucius must have had in mind the law of retaliation when he stated the Golden Rule philosophy in about this way, 'Do not unto others that which you would not have them do unto you.'

And he might well have added an explanation to the effect that the reason for his injunction was based upon the common tendency of man to retaliate in kind.

Those who do not understand the law upon which the Golden Rule is based are inclined to argue that it will not work, for the reason that men are inclined toward the principle of exacting 'an eye for an eye and a tooth for a tooth', which is nothing more nor less than the law of retaliation. If they would go a step further in their reasoning, they would understand that they are looking at the *negative* effects of this law, and that the self-same law is capable of producing *positive* effects as well.

In other words, if you would not have your own eye plucked out, then insure against this misfortune by refraining from plucking out the other fellow's eye. Go a step further and render the other fellow an act of kindly, helpful service, and *through the operation of this same law of retaliation* he will render you a similar service.

And, if he should fail to reciprocate your kindness— what then?

You have profited, nevertheless, because of the effect of your act on *your own sub-conscious mind!*

Thus by indulging in acts of kindness and applying, always, the Golden Rule philosophy, you are sure of benefit from one source and at the same time you have a pretty fair chance of profiting from another source.

It might happen that you would base all of your acts toward others on the Golden Rule without enjoying any direct reciprocation for a long period of time, and it might so happen that those to whom you rendered those acts of kindness would never reciprocate, but meantime you have been adding vitality to your own character and sooner or later this *positive character* which you have been building will begin to assert itself and you will discover that you have been receiving compound interest on compound interest in return for those acts of kindness which appeared to have been wasted on those who neither appreciated nor reciprocated them.

Remember that your *reputation* is made by others, but your *character* is made by *you!*

You want your reputation to be a favourable one, but you cannot be sure that it will be for the reason that it is something that exists outside of your own control, in the minds of others.

It is what others believe you to be. With your character it is different. Your character is that which *you are,* as the results of your *thoughts* and *deeds.* You control it. You can make it weak, good or bad. When you are satisfied and know in your mind that your character is above reproach you need not worry about your reputation, for it is as impossible for your character to be destroyed or damaged by anyone except yourself as it is to destroy matter or energy.

It was this truth that Emerson had in mind when he said, 'A political victory, a rise of rents, the recovery of your sick or the return of your absent friend, or some other quite external event raises your spirits, and you think your days are prepared for you. *Do not believe it.* It can never be so. *Nothing can bring you peace but yourself. Nothing can bring you peace but the triumph of principles.'*

One reason for being just toward others is the fact that such action may cause them to reciprocate, in kind, but a better reason is the fact that kindness and justice toward others develop *positive character* in all who indulge in these acts.

You may withhold from me the reward to which I am entitled for rendering you helpful service, but no one can deprive me of the benefit I will derive from the rendering of that service in so far as it adds to my own *character.*

POINTS TO REMEMBER

1. The Golden Rule means to do unto others as you would wish them to do unto you.
2. What you sow, you shall reap.
3. No man can attain success in its highest form without the aid of earnest prayer!

www.ingramcontent.com/pod-product-compliance
Lightning Source LLC
Chambersburg PA
CBHW030219170426
43194CB00007BA/800